Table of Contents

I0427594

General Notes

1.   All years referred to are fiscal years, unless otherwise noted.

2.   Detail in this document may not add to the totals due to rounding.

Introduction

Major Savings and Reforms in the President's 2009 Budget

> *"As we work to keep taxes low, we must do more to restrain spending. My Budget proposes to keep non-security discretionary spending growth below 1 percent for 2009 and then hold it at that level for the next 4 years. It also cuts spending on projects that are not achieving results—because good intentions alone do not justify a program that is not working."*
>
> President George W. Bush
> The Budget Message of the President
> Fiscal Year 2009 Budget

This volume describes and provides funding levels for major discretionary and mandatory savings and reform proposals in the Fiscal Year 2009 Budget. These proposals will result in savings to taxpayers and improved Government services by eliminating or restructuring low-priority programs and programs that are not producing results. The proposals were guided by criteria that considered whether the programs met the Nation's priorities, constituted an appropriate and effective use of taxpayer resources by the Federal Government, and produced the intended results.

In total, the Budget proposes to terminate or reduce 151 discretionary programs, reducing 2009 spending by $18 billion. These include 103 terminations saving $7 billion and 48 reductions saving $11 billion. The Budget also proposes mandatory spending reforms that will achieve an additional $16 billion in net savings in 2009, and result in $208 billion in savings through 2013. Mandatory savings proposals highlighted in this volume total $19 billion in 2009 and $233 billion through 2013, and exclude reforms that are cost-neutral or result in cost increases.

The Budget also includes a number of budget reform proposals which are described in the Analytical Perspectives volume at:
http://www.budget.gov/budget/fy2009/pdf/apers/proposals.pdf

Discretionary Terminations

Discretionary Program Terminations
(Budget authority and obligation limitations in millions of dollars)

	2008 Enacted	2009 Request	2009 Less 2008
Program Terminations			
Department of Agriculture:			
Community Connect (Broadband) Grants	13	---	-13
Community Facility Grants	27	---	-27
Economic Impact Grants	14	---	-14
Farm Labor Housing Program	22	---	-22
Food and Nutrition Service - Commodity Supplemental Food Program	139	---	-139
Forest Service Economic Action	4	---	-4
Forest Service Valles Caldera National Preserve	4	---	-4
High Cost Energy Grants	20	---	-20
Rural Economic Development Loan and Grant Program	---	-39	-39
Multifamily Housing Direct Loans	30	---	-30
Public Broadcast Grants	5	---	-5
Research and Extension Grant Earmarks/Low Priority Programs	144	---	-144
Resource Conservation and Development Program	51	---	-51
Rural Business Grants	45	---	-45
Section 9006, Renewable Energy Program	36	---	-36
Self-Help Housing Grants	39	---	-39
Single Family Housing Direct Loans	105	---	-105
Value Added Producer Grants	19	---	-19
Watershed Programs	30	---	-30
Total, Department of Agriculture	**747**	**-39**	**-786**
Department of Commerce:			
Emergency Steel Guarantee Loan Program	---	-49	-49
Manufacturing Extension Partnership	90	4	-86
Public Telecommunications Facilities, Planning and Construction Grants	19	---	-19
Technology Innovation Program	46	---	-46
Total, Department of Commerce	**155**	**-45**	**-200**
Department of Education:			
Academies for American History and Civics	2	---	-2
Advanced Credentialing	10	---	-10
Alaska Native Education Equity	33	---	-33
Alcohol Abuse Reduction	32	---	-32
Arts in Education	38	---	-38
B.J. Stupak Olympic Scholarships	1	---	-1
Byrd Honors Scholarships	40	---	-40
Career and Technical Education National Programs	8	---	-8
Career and Technical Education State Grants	1,161	---	-1,161
Civic Education	32	---	-32
Close-Up Fellowships	2	---	-2
Comprehensive School Reform	2	---	-2
Education for Native Hawaiians	33	---	-33
Educational Technology State Grants	267	---	-267
Elementary and Secondary School Counseling	49	---	-49
Even Start	66	---	-66
Excellence in Economic Education	1	---	-1
Foundations for Learning	1	---	-1
Higher Education Demonstrations for Students with Disabilities	7	---	-7
Historic Whaling and Trading Partners	9	---	-9
Javits Gifted and Talented Education	7	---	-7
Leveraging Educational Assistance Programs	64	---	-64
Mental Health Integration in Schools	5	---	-5
Mentoring Program	49	---	-49
National Writing Project	24	---	-24
Parental Assistance Information Centers	39	---	-39
Perkins Loan Cancellations	64	---	-64
Physical Education	76	---	-76
Projects with Industry	19	---	-19
Reading is Fundamental	25	---	-25

Discretionary Program Terminations
(Budget authority and obligation limitations in millions of dollars)

	2008 Enacted	2009 Request	2009 Less 2008
Ready to Teach	11	---	-11
School Leadership	14	---	-14
Smaller Learning Communities	80	---	-80
Special Olympics Education Programs	12	---	-12
State Grants for Incarcerated Youth	22	---	-22
Strengthening Alaska Native/Native Hawaiian Institutions	12	---	-12
Supplemental Educational Opportunity Grants	757	---	-757
Supported Employment State Grants	29	---	-29
Teacher Quality Enhancement	34	---	-34
Teachers for a Competitive Tomorrow	2	---	-2
Tech-Prep Education State Grants	103	---	-103
Thurgood Marshall Legal Opportunity	3	---	-3
Tr bally Controlled Postsecondary Vocational Education	8	---	-8
Underground Railroad Program	2	---	-2
Vocation Rehabilitation - Migrant and Seasonal Farmworkers	2	---	-2
Vocation Rehabilitation - Recreational Programs	2	---	-2
Women's Educational Equity	2	---	-2
Total, Department of Education	**3,261**	**---**	**-3,261**
Department of Energy:			
Oil and Gas Research and Development	25	---	-25
University Nuclear Energy Program (Nuclear Regulatory Commission)	15	---	-15
Weatherization Assistance Program*	227	---	-227
Total, Department of Energy	**267**	**---**	**-267**
Department of Health and Human Services:			
Administration for Children and Families - Community Services Block Grant	654	---	-654
Administration for Children and Families - Other Community Service Programs	45	---	-45
Administration for Aging - Alzheimer's Demonstration Project	11	---	-11
Administration for Aging - Preventive Health Services	21	---	-21
Centers for Disease Control - Preventive Health and Health Services Block Grant	97	---	-97
Congressional Earmarks	451	---	-451
HRSA - Children's Hospital Graduate Medical Education Payments	302	---	-302
HRSA - Maternal and Child Health Small Categorical Grants	40	---	-40
Indian Health Service - Urban Indian Health Program	35	---	-35
Total, Department of Health and Human Services	**1,656**	**---**	**-1,656**
Department of Housing and Urban Development:			
Brownfields	10	---	-10
Revitalization of Severely Depressed Public Housing (HOPE VI)	100	---	-100
Rural Housing and Economic Development	17	---	-17
Section 108 Loan Program	5	---	-5
Total, Department of Housing and Urban Development	**132**	**---**	**-132**
Department of the Interior:			
Bureau of Indian Affairs - Housing Improvement Program	14	---	-14
Bureau of Indian Affairs - Johnson-O'Malley Assistance Grants	21	---	-21
Indian Land Consolidation Program	10	---	-10
Land and Water Conservation Fund State Recreation Grants	25	---	-25
National Park Service Statutory Aid	7	---	-7
Office of Surface Mining Reclamation Grants	20	---	-20
Rural Fire Assistance Program	6	---	-6
Total, Department of the Interior	**103**	**---**	**-103**
Department of Justice:			
State Criminal Alien Assistance Program	410	---	-410
Total, Department of Justice	**410**	**---**	**-410**

Discretionary Program Terminations

(Budget authority and obligation limitations in millions of dollars)

	2008 Enacted	2009 Request	2009 Less 2008
Department of Labor:			
Denali Commission Job Training Earmark	7	---	-7
Migrant and Seasonal Farmworkers Training Program	80	---	-80
Susan Harwood Training Grants..	10	---	-10
Work Incentive Grants	14	---	-14
Total, Department of Labor	**111**	**---**	**-111**
Environmental Protection Agency:			
Targeted Watershed Grants	10	---	-10
Unrequested Water Infrastructure Projects	133	---	-133
Total, Environment Protection Agency	**143**	**---**	**-143**
Other Agencies:			
Commission of Fine Arts, National Capital Arts and Cultural Affairs	8	---	-8
National Veterans Business Development Corporation	1	---	-1
Postal Service Forgone Revenue Appropriation	29	---	-29
Total, Other Agencies	**38**	**---**	**-38**
Total, Program Terminations	**7,023**	**-84**	**-7,107**

* In Table S-5, Discretionary Program Termination and Reductions, of the main *Budget* volume, 2008 Enacted for the Weatherization Assistance Program was reported incorrectly as $243 million. The correct figure, $227 million, is displayed above.

Department of Agriculture: Discretionary Proposal
Community Connect (Broadband) Grants

Funding Summary
(In millions of dollars)

	2008 Enacted	2009 Proposed	Change From 2008
Budget Authority........................	13	---	-13

Administration Proposal and Impact

The Budget proposes zero funding for Community Connect Broadband grants. However, funds are available through the Rural Utilities Service's (RUS') broadband loan program to provide broadband service to rural areas. It is more efficient to support broadband service through loans rather than grants because the appropriations need only cover the risk the borrowers will default. Communities can obtain loans through RUS, which, due to the low interest, the communities are able to repay.

Background

The purpose of the Community Connect Broadband Grant Program is to provide broadband transmission service that fosters economic growth and delivers enhanced educational, health care, and public safety services. Grants would be used for the deployment of broadband transmission service to extremely rural, lower-income communities on a "community-oriented connectivity" basis. This program is duplicative of the Broadband Loan Program authorized in the 2002 Farm Bill. The areas eligible for grants are also eligible for low-cost broadband loans through RUS.

Department of Agriculture: Discretionary Proposal
Community Facilities Grant

Funding Summary
(In millions of dollars)

	2008 Enacted	2009 Proposed	Change From 2008
Budget Authority..........................	27	---	-27

Administration Proposal and Impact

The Budget proposes no funding for the Community Facilities (CF) Grant Program. Thirty-five percent of the funds are earmarked; also, the program's second evaluation under the Program Assessment Rating Tool revealed that the grants are not always used in conjunction with the community facilities direct loans. Therefore, the CF grants are redundant with other Federal economic development programs. While the grants are redundant, the loans are not, and the community facilities direct and guaranteed loan programs continue to be fully funded in the President's Budget.

Background

The CF Grant Program was newly authorized in the 1996 Farm Bill. It was to be used in conjunction with the community facilities direct loan program or as a stand-alone grant to provide financial assistance for essential community facilities, such as health care, public safety, and educational/cultural services. The grants are for rural areas, defined as communities less than 20,000.

Department of Agriculture: Discretionary Proposal
Economic Impact Grants

Funding Summary
(In millions of dollars)

	2008 Enacted	2009 Proposed	Change From 2008
Budget Authority........................	14	---	-14

Administration Proposal and Impact

The Budget proposes no funding for the Economic Impact Grants Program, which are a special category of community facilities grant designed for areas of high unemployment and out-migration. Like many other economic and community grant programs, this program is redundant with other Federal programs.

Background

Economic Impact Grants were authorized in the Grain Standards and Warehouse Improvement Act of 2000. This is a specialized community facilities grant program that requires that the community be suffering from extreme unemployment and/or severe economic depression in addition to being rural and lacking the ability to secure commercial credit. It may be used in conjunction with the community facilities direct loan program but is typically a stand alone grant to provide financial assistance for essential community facilities, such as health care, public safety, and educational/cultural services. Rural areas for this program are defined as communities of less than 20,000.

Department of Agriculture: Discretionary Proposal
Farm Labor Housing Program

Funding Summary
(In millions of dollars)

	2008 Enacted	2009 Proposed	Change From 2008
Budget Authority............................	22	---	-22
Grant BA plus Loan Level..........	37	---	-37

Administration Proposal and Impact

The 2009 Budget requests no funding for the Farm Labor Housing Direct Loan and Grant program. Farm Labor Housing is a special category of multifamily housing specifically for farm laborers. Like the multifamily housing direct loan program, the structure of the Farm Labor Housing program is costly and inefficient. Developers interested in constructing a farm labor housing project qualify for the Department's multifamily guaranteed loan program.

Background

The Farm Labor Housing Loan and Grant Program, authorized in the Housing Act of 1949, provides capital financing for the development of housing for domestic farm laborers. A direct loan/grant combination is provided to construct, rehabilitate, and/or repair multifamily rural rental housing for very low- and low-income migrant farm laborers. To help achieve affordable rents, the interest rate is subsidized to one percent, and, in addition, the farm worker's rents are further reduced to 30 percent of their adjusted income through rental assistance grants.

The Administration has proposed no funding for new construction in the multifamily housing direct loan program since 2001. This was necessary to focus on rehabilitating the current portfolio and discontinuing a program that is costly and inefficient. The reduction in funding was continued and expanded beginning in 2007 by requesting no funding for construction of any kind for the multifamily housing direct loan program. Taking the next step to not fund the Farm Labor Housing further expands on that policy. However, the loan level for the multifamily guaranteed loan program is increased by more than $170 million to $300 million for 2009.

Department of Agriculture: Discretionary Proposal
Commodity Supplemental Food Program

Funding Summary
(In millions of dollars)

	2008 Enacted	2009 Proposed	Change From 2008
Budget Authority.........................	139	---	-139

Administration Proposal and Impact

The 2009 Budget proposes to eliminate the Commodity Supplemental Food Program (CSFP). In the limited areas where it is available, the program duplicates two of the Nation's largest Federal nutrition assistance programs – Food Stamps and the Special Supplemental Nutrition Program for Women, Infants and Children (WIC). Instead, the 2009 Budget provides funding to serve all eligible individuals who apply for WIC, and provides resources for outreach and temporary benefits to help elderly households transition from CSFP to the Food Stamp Program.

Background

CSFP provides a monthly food package to low-income women, infants, children and elderly in selected sites in 32 States and the District of Columbia, and on two Indian reservations. Many recipients are eligible for the Food Stamp and WIC programs. By contrast, those programs provide nationwide access to generally larger and more flexible nutrition benefits for all eligible individuals who apply.

Department of Agriculture: Discretionary Proposal
Forest Service Economic Action Program

Funding Summary
(In millions of dollars)

	2008 Enacted	2009 Proposed	Change From 2008
Budget Authority.........................	4	---	-4

Administration Proposal and Impact

The Budget proposes to terminate the Forest Service's Economic Action Program. This program duplicates the efforts of other Department of Agriculture (USDA) Rural Development programs that can more effectively address priority needs in rural areas and assist forest-based industries. In addition, the President's Healthy Forests Initiative calls for significant increases in stewardship contracting that will benefit local businesses by allowing private companies, communities, and others to retain forest and rangeland products in exchange for the service of thinning trees and brush and removing dead wood. This approach fosters a public/private partnership to restore forest and rangeland health by giving those who undertake the contract the ability to invest in equipment and infrastructure.

Background

The Economic Action Program provides technical and financial assistance to communities and groups to enhance rural economies through the utilization of forest and related natural resources. Established by the 1990 Farm Bill, the Economic Action Program is highly earmarked by the Congress and is duplicative of other programs within USDA.

Department of Agriculture: Discretionary Proposal
Forest Service Valles Caldera National Preserve

Funding Summary
(In millions of dollars)

	2008 Enacted	2009 Proposed	Change From 2008
Budget Authority........................	4	---	-4

Administration Proposal and Impact

The Budget proposes to terminate funding for the Valles Caldera National Preserve. The 2008 funding completes the Preserve's move toward financial self-sufficiency as envisioned by the authorizing legislation. Other funding is also available to the Preserve through receipts generated from hunting, fishing, recreation, grazing, and other uses.

Background

The Valles Caldera Preservation Act of 2000 (P.L. 106-248) provided for the acquisition of the Baca Ranch, located in the Jemez Mountains of New Mexico. The Act requires management of the Preserve by the Valles Caldera Trust (VCT), a wholly-owned Government corporation. The Act provides for interim management of the Preserve by the Forest Service with appropriated funds until the Trust assumes full responsibility for the Preserve. The Trust assumed management authority over the Preserve in August 2002.

The Preserve was established to protect various natural resources within its boundaries, and for providing multiple-use and sustained yield of renewable resources within the Preserve. Receipts are derived through multiple uses of the Preserve, including hunting, fishing, recreation, and grazing.

Department of Agriculture: Discretionary Proposal
High Cost Energy Grant Program

Funding Summary
(In millions of dollars)

	2008 Enacted	2009 Proposed	Change From 2008
Budget Authority........................	20	---	-20

Administration Proposal and Impact

The Budget proposes no new funding for High Cost Energy grants, because such grants are less effective than other forms of assistance. In particular, funds available through the Rural Utilities Service's (RUS) electric loan program are used to support the provision of electric service in high-cost areas. However, using loans to provide support is less expensive than using grants because loans provide more support (loan level) with fewer appropriated dollars. Low interest loans through RUS would also help lower-utility rates.

Background

High Cost Energy grants are for areas where the cost to deliver energy is significantly higher than the national average. The grants fund energy facilities and more cost effective means of acquiring fuel in extremely high energy cost communities. Only Alaska, Hawaii, the territories, and a few isolated areas within the continental United States qualify for the program. The goals of the High Cost Energy Grant program are duplicative of the RUS electric loan program, which is more effective. The areas eligible for grants are also eligible for low cost electric loans through RUS.

Department of Agriculture: Discretionary Proposal
Rural Economic Development Loan and Grant Program

Funding Summary
(In millions of dollars)

	2008 Enacted	2009 Proposed	Change From 2008
Budget Authority........................	---	-39	-39

Administration Proposal and Impact

The Budget proposes to cancel $39 million in unneeded funding for lower-priority and duplicative programs authorized by pending farm legislation. An additional $603 million is proposed in discretionary reductions. The program assists electric and telephone utilities to promote sustainable rural economic development and job creation projects. In the past, the Congress has adopted similar savings proposed by the Administration.

Background

This program provides grants to utilities for rural economic development and job creation projects. Funding for this program is provided from the interest differential on the Rural Utilities Service (RUS) borrower's cushion of credit accounts. Funding for this mandatory program is determined by the amount of interest collected on the loans of RUS borrowers. The Budget proposes to cancel the full amount of the projected interest, providing an offset to fund higher-priority discretionary programs.

Department of Agriculture: Discretionary Proposal
Multifamily Housing Direct Loan Program

Funding Summary
(In millions of dollars)

	2008 Enacted	2009 Proposed	Change From 2008
Budget Authority........................	30	---	-30
Loan Level.................................	70	---	-70

Administration Proposal and Impact

The Budget proposes no funding for the Multifamily Housing Direct Loan Program. Instead, the Administration proposes to provide rural multifamily housing units through the multifamily housing loan guarantee program. This will allow the Department to provide a similar number of units at a lower cost. The loan level for the multifamily guaranteed loan program is increased by more than $170 million to $300 million for 2009.

Background

The Multifamily Housing Direct Loan Program, authorized in the Housing Act of 1949, provides capital financing for the development of housing for very low- and low-income, elderly or handicapped residents. The program makes loans to private developers or nonprofits to construct, rehabilitate, and/or repair multifamily rental housing in rural areas. To help achieve affordable rents, the interest rate is subsidized to one percent, and, in addition, the tenant's rents are further reduced to 30 percent of their adjusted income through rental assistance grants.

Since 2001, the Administration has not requested funding for new construction in this program, because the higher-priority focus has been to deal with dilapidation in the current portfolio. The dilapidation issue arose because the original loan agreement did not require adequate reserves for major property improvements. In addition, these loans are for 50 years and pre-payment is prohibited.

Department of Agriculture: Discretionary Proposal
Public Broadcasting Grants

Funding Summary
(In millions of dollars)

	2008 Enacted	2009 Proposed	Change From 2008
Budget Authority….....................	5	---	-5

Administration Proposal and Impact

The Budget proposes no new funding for Public Broadcast grants. Funds provided in previous years will already have helped public broadcast companies convert to digital prior to the February 2009 deadline.

Background

The purpose of the Public Broadcast Grant Program is to provide funding to public broadcast companies to convert to digital. Funds have been provided for this program for five years. With the deadline of February 2009, funding made available in 2009 would be too late to benefit the companies.

Department of Agriculture: Discretionary Proposal
Research and Extension Grants and Low Priority Programs

Funding Summary
(In millions of dollars)

	2008 Enacted	2009 Proposed	Change From 2008
Budget Authority..........................	144	---	-144

Administration Proposal and Impact

The Budget proposes to terminate funding enacted in 2008 for over 200 unrequested research and extension grants and low-priority projects. These grants are not awarded on the basis of a competitive, merit-reviewed process and do not represent the most effective use of Federal dollars. The Budget redirects a portion of these funds to the Department of Agriculture's National Research Initiative – its main discretionary competitive grants program.

Background

The Administration's policy has been to support research funding that is awarded on a competitive peer-reviewed basis as the most effective use of taxpayer dollars. A prime example is the National Research Initiative, for which increases have been proposed in recent years. At the same time, the Budget proposes to eliminate funding for earmarks and low-priority programs enacted in the previous year, since they are not awarded on a competitive basis and often support State and local needs, rather than address national issues. Earmarks also reduce the Administration's ability to effectively manage program allocations.

Department of Agriculture: Discretionary Proposal
Resource Conservation and Development Program

Funding Summary
(In millions of dollars)

	2008 Enacted	2009 Proposed	Change From 2008
Budget Authority......................	51	---	-51

Administration Action

The Budget proposes to eliminate the Resource Conservation and Development (RC&D) program. A Program Assessment Rating Tool evaluation determined that the program is duplicative. It concluded that the program duplicates other similar resource conservation planning, rural economic development, and community programs provided by other Department of Agriculture agencies (such as the Forest Service and Rural Development) and other Federal departments, such as the Department of Commerce's Economic Development Administration. The Budget instead targets scarce conservation funding to well-defined programs with the highest conservation outcomes.

Background

RC&D provides assistance to local communities to address locally identified natural resource and development concerns. The program aims to improve community access to Federal conservation and community development assistance and develop local community leadership. RC&D's long-term goal is to improve the capability of local communities to plan and deliver improvement projects. These include not only natural resource projects, but also projects for economic development, community infrastructure, waste collection and disposal, and recreation and tourism.

Several other Federal programs provide assistance to communities for these purposes. It is also unclear what role RC&D plays in implementing NRCS' mission that is not already filled by NRCS' State Technical Committees, which have substantial collaborative relationships with State and local resource agencies outside of the RC&D program.

Department of Agriculture: Discretionary Proposal
Rural Business Grants

Funding Summary
(In millions of dollars)

	2008 Enacted	2009 Proposed	Change From 2008
Budget Authority......................	45	---	-45

Administration Proposal and Impact

The Budget proposes no funding for Rural Business Enterprise Grants and Rural Business Opportunity Grants. These programs are duplicative of other Department of Agriculture rural development programs and Federal programs in the Departments of Commerce, Health and Human Services, Housing and Urban Development, and the Treasury. In addition, the effectiveness of these programs is limited because they are traditionally earmarked.

Background

Rural Business Enterprise Grants are authorized in the Consolidated Farm and Rural Development Act of 1972; the Rural Business Opportunity Grants are authorized in the Federal Agriculture Improvement and Reform Act of 1996. The Rural Business Enterprise Grants program provides grants to public bodies, private nonprofit corporations, and federally-recognized Indian tribal groups to assist emerging businesses in rural communities. The Rural Business Opportunity Grants program funds economic planning for rural communities, technical assistance for rural businesses, and training for rural entrepreneurs or economic development officials.

Department of Agriculture: Discretionary Proposal
Section 9006, Renewable Energy Program

Funding Summary
(In millions of dollars)

	2008 Enacted	2009 Proposed	Change From 2008
Budget Authority......................	36	---	-36

Administration Proposal and Impact

The Budget proposes no discretionary funding for the Renewable Energy Program because the Budget includes a mandatory proposal to fund this program. The Administration's Farm Bill proposal requests $50 million for grants and $21 million for loans, which is a $35 million increase over 2008 enacted levels.

Background

Created in the 2002 Farm Bill, the Renewable Energy Systems and Energy Efficiency Improvement Program provides funds for businesses and farmers in rural communities to produce renewable energy and obtain energy efficiencies. The program distributes grants and loans to entities in rural communities of 50,000 or less. The Administration's Farm Bill proposal requests $21 million for loans and $50 million for grants. Loans would target additional projects, including cellulosic ethanol plants and be capped at $100 million; currently they are capped at $10 million. Grants would be targeted to smaller alternative energy and energy efficient projects.

Department of Agriculture: Discretionary Proposal
Self-Help Housing Grants

Funding Summary
(In millions of dollars)

	2008 Enacted	2009 Proposed	Change From 2008
Budget Authority..........................	39	---	-39

Administration Proposal and Impact

The Budget proposes no funding for Self-Help Housing Grants. Demand for the program also relies heavily on the funding of the Department's direct Single Family Housing Direct Loan Program, for which the Administration is requesting no 2009 funds. Historically 98 percent of these grant recipients qualify and receive single family direct loans from the Department of Agriculture. With the termination of the direct single family housing program there is no need to fund this program.

Background

This program provides financial assistance to nonprofit organizations that offer technical assistance to low- and very low-income households to build their own homes in a rural area. Funds may be used to pay salaries, rent, and office expenses of the nonprofit organization under this program, and it provides some families their only homeownership opportunity. However, most such families are very low-income, minority families and nearly all obtain Department of Agriculture direct single family housing loans.

Department of Agriculture: Discretionary Proposal
Single Family Housing Direct Loans

Funding Summary
(In millions of dollars)

	2008 Enacted	2009 Proposed	Change From 2008
Budget Authority..........................	105	---	-105
Program Level............................	1,121	---	-1,121

Administration Proposal and Impact

The Budget proposes no funding for the Single Family Housing Direct Loan Program, since the most cost-effective way to provide single family housing mortgage assistance is through guaranteed loans. The single family housing guaranteed loan program was newly authorized in 1990 at $100 million and has grown to more than $3 billion annually. Meanwhile, the single family direct loan program has been stagnant at approximately a $1 billion loan level.

The shift toward guaranteed loans has also occurred with other Federal homeownership programs; in fact, there are now no Federal single family direct loan home ownership programs for urban areas. While some rural areas remain isolated from broad credit availability, these areas are shrinking as broadband internet access and on-line lending grow. Therefore, relying on the private banking industry to provide this service, with a guarantee from the Federal Government, is a more efficient way to deliver rural homeownership assistance.

To compensate for the elimination of funding for direct single family housing loans, the Budget proposes a $4.8 billion guaranteed single family housing loan level, an increase of over $600 million above 2008.

Background

The Single Family Housing Direct Loan Program, authorized in the Housing Act of 1949, provides loans that are directly funded by the Government to help low-income individuals or households purchase homes in rural areas. Families must currently be without adequate housing, but be able to afford the mortgage payments, including taxes and insurance. In addition, interest payment subsidies are available to applicants to enhance their ability to repay the loans. The interest rate is based on the borrower's income and can be subsidized to as low as one percent, but it is capped at the Government's borrowing rate. Applicants must be unable to obtain credit elsewhere, yet have reasonable credit histories.

Department of Agriculture: Discretionary Proposal
Value Added Producer Grants

Funding Summary
(In millions of dollars)

	2008 Enacted	2009 Proposed	Change From 2008
Budget Authority.....................	19	---	-19

Administration Proposal and Impact

The Budget proposes no funding for Value Added Producer Grants. Performance measures indicate that the program is ineffective and inefficient. Less than 30 percent of assisted businesses are still operational three years after the project is completed, and only 48 percent of grants are fully spent within 18 months of the obligation date (the grants are designed to be fully utilized within a one-year time period).

Background

The Value Added Producer Grant Program was created in the 2002 Farm Bill. Grants may be used for planning activities, for working capital for marketing value-added agricultural products, and for farm-based renewable energy. Eligible applicants are independent producers, farmer and rancher cooperatives, agricultural producer groups, and majority-controlled producer-based business ventures located in communities of 50,000 people or less.

Department of Agriculture: Discretionary Proposal
Watershed and Flood Prevention Operations

Funding Summary
(In millions of dollars)

	2008 Enacted	2009 Proposed	Change From 2008
Budget Authority........................	30	---	-30

Administration Proposal and Impact

The Budget proposes to terminate the Natural Resources Conservation Service's (NRCS') Watershed Protection and Flood Prevention Operations Program. The program funds local, in many cases privately-owned, flood prevention and water improvement projects that are not Federal priorities. Moreover, extensive congressional earmarking in this program effectively prevents NRCS from identifying and funding priority projects; for example, the 2008 Consolidated Appropriations Act earmarked 100 percent of the funds for 25 congressionally-directed projects. A 2004 Program Assessment Rating Tool evaluation of this program also found that NRCS's typical flood damage reduction project provided about 50 percent less net benefits than a typical Federal Emergency Management Agency (FEMA) project and about 70 percent less net benefits than a typical Army Corps project (though many of NRCS's projects address a broader array of resource issues such as water quality, water supply, and rehabilitation). The Budget proposes no funding for this program and redirecting the savings to other higher priority programs.

Background

The Watershed Operations program provides technical and financial assistance to local communities to plan, design, and construct flood prevention, water supply, and water quality improvement projects. The program is designed to operate in federally-authorized watershed project areas that are up to 250,000 acres in size. In addition, each project must contain benefits directly related to agriculture that account for at least 20 percent of the total benefits. By agreement with the Army Corps of Engineers, this program funds only operations in small, rural watersheds and in communities with small populations. NRCS has helped to construct thousands of dams and other flood control projects across the country over the program's 60-year history. NRCS has reported that there is a "backlog" of $1.4 billion in requests from local communities for new community watershed and flood prevention projects. However, these projects should be a local rather than a Federal responsibility.

In the 2004 Budget, OMB compared the cost effectiveness of the Corps of Engineers, NRCS, and FEMA flood damage reduction programs. Evaluation of projects completed over a five-year period demonstrated that NRCS' program provided the fewest benefits per dollar.

Department of Commerce: Discretionary Proposal
Emergency Steel Guaranteed Loan Program

Funding Summary
(In millions of dollars)

	2008 Enacted	2009 Proposed	Change From 2008
Budget Authority.........................	---	-49	-49

Administration Proposal and Impact

The Budget proposes to cancel all remaining credit subsidy balances for the Emergency Steel Guaranteed Loan Program (ESGLP), as the subsidized financing assistance that these funds support is no longer needed, due to the recovery of the industry.

Background

The ESGLP was enacted in 1999 to help steel firms suffering financial losses from low prices and the inability to obtain financing for continued operations and facility re-investment. Since 2003, the Administration has proposed to cancel funds from the program as it has become an unwarranted corporate subsidy and exposes taxpayers to significant costs from loan guarantee defaults. Further, demand for guarantees has been much lower than expected. Only three loans have been made through the program, and no new loans have been guaranteed since 2003.

Beginning in 2004, international demand for steel increased significantly and numerous consolidations occurred in the domestic steel production market. According to the Bureau of Labor Statistics' Producer Price Index, steel mill product prices are 67 percent higher than in 2003 and 73 percent higher than in 1999, when the program was enacted. The industry's recovery is further evidence that this program is no longer needed.

Department of Commerce: Discretionary Proposal
Hollings Manufacturing Extension Program (MEP)

Funding Summary
(In millions of dollars)

	2008 Enacted	2009 Proposed	Change From 2008
Budget Authority..........................	90	4	-86

Administration Proposal and Impact

The Budget proposes that Federal funding for MEP centers be discontinued, and that they become self-supporting, as intended in the program's original authorization. Requested funds in 2009 will be used to cover termination costs.

MEP centers provide manufacturing firms consulting services that are also provided by private entities. Given the reported benefits MEP clients receive from the program, they have the profit incentive and means to cover the costs of these services through modestly increased fees.

Although intended to benefit small firms, MEP centers also assist larger firms. These firms often use outside providers of legal, accounting, and other services and should not require federally-subsidized management consulting services.

Background

The MEP program was established in 1988 to provide business and technical assistance services to small- and medium-sized manufacturers. MEP's original legislated design called for a phase-out of Federal monies to each center after six years of funding, with the goal of making each center self sufficient. While this requirement was removed in 1998, all centers are now more than six years old, and the average center is 13 years old.

Currently, fees charged to recipients generally cover one-third of the centers' costs; the Federal Government and State/local matching grants together cover the remaining two-thirds of the costs.

Department of Commerce: Discretionary Proposal
Public Telecommunications Facilities, Planning and Construction Grants

Funding Summary
(In millions of dollars)

	2008 Enacted	2009 Proposed	Change From 2008
Budget Authority..........................	19	---	-19

Administration Proposal and Impact

Since 2000, most Public Telecommunications Facilities Planning (PTFP) awards have supported public television stations' conversion to digital broadcasting. Digital conversion efforts mandated by the Federal Communications Commission are now largely complete, and there is no further need for this program.

Background

PTFP was created in the early 1960s to assist in the planning and construction of public telecommunications facilities through matching grants of up to 75 percent of project costs. The Commerce Department's National Telecommunications and Information Administration has administered the program since 1979.

Since 2000, almost 70 percent of PTFP awards have supported public television stations' conversion to digital broadcasting prior to the February 2009 deadline.

Department of Commerce: Discretionary Proposal
Technology Innovation Program (TIP)

Funding Summary
(In millions of dollars)

	2008 Enacted	2009 Proposed	Change From 2008
Budget Authority.........................	46	---	-46

Administration Proposal and Impact

The Administration supported the recent termination of the Advanced Technology Program (ATP) by the Congress, but believes that the Technology Innovation Program (TIP) that was created in its place is not warranted in today's research and development environment, given the growth of venture capital and other financing sources for high-tech projects.

While TIP is intended to be a better targeted program than ATP, the Administration believes that it will still provide subsidies for activities that private industry has the means and incentive to support.

The Budget continues the Administration's support for basic scientific research through the American Competitiveness Initiative (ACI), which doubles over 10 years the collective budget of ACI programs at the National Science Foundation, the Department of Energy's Office of Science, and Commerce's National Institute of Standards and Technology labs.

Background

ATP was a grant program for businesses that was intended to develop new technologies for commercial use. TIP was created in the 2007 America COMPETES Act and is intended to be more focused on national needs. However, it is a lower priority for Federal funding than basic research and agencies' mission-directed research programs.

Department of Education: Discretionary Proposal
Small Elementary and Secondary Education Programs

Funding Summary
(In millions of dollars)

	2008 Enacted	2009 Proposed	Change From 2009
Budget Authority..........................	494	---	-494

Administration Proposal and Impact

The Budget proposes to terminate 23 small elementary and secondary education grant programs. Termination of these narrow-purpose programs does not mean that Federal support is no longer available for these activities. States and school districts that view these issues as a high priority can support them with funds provided under broad-purpose Federal education programs, such as Title I, Teacher Quality State Grants, and other programs.

Background

The 23 grant programs described below are narrow-purpose and have no demonstrated results. Many of the activities supported by these programs can be supported under large formula grants if localities determine the need to be pressing. Others support activities targeted for elimination that do not fill an appropriate Federal role. While most of these programs are intended to support laudable purposes, their design has not allowed them to meet their goals. Many of them lack performance objectives and measures and none have rigorous evaluations, preventing the Department of Education from assessing program effectiveness and identifying successful intervention strategies that could have broad national impact. Further, most of these programs lack administrative mechanisms for holding grantees accountable for achieving results, and programs are required by statute to be awarded to specific service providers rather than running true competitions. These programs differ from many other programs authorized under the Elementary and Secondary Education Act of 1965 (ESEA), such as Title I and Reading First, which have a strong accountability framework and encourage the use of scientifically based interventions, improving the prospects for participants to achieve positive and measurable outcomes.

Most of these programs are authorized by the ESEA and are subject to reauthorization this year. The Administration is not recommending reauthorization for any of these programs.

Comprehensive School Reform (CSR) (2008 level: $1.6 million) supports research-based reform models that address multiple aspects of schools and instruction, particularly in low-performing schools. In 2004, the Department of Education and the Office of Management and Budget (OMB) used the Program Assessment Rating Tool (PART) to assess the program and found it to be duplicative of several aspects of Title I Grants to Local Educational Agencies, the largest ESEA program. It also duplicates School Improvement grants, both of which can fund comprehensive reforms. In 2006, the Congress reduced funding for this program by $197 million, providing only a few million dollars to complete the contract for the program's technical assistance center. The last year for that contract is 2008; therefore, no additional funds are needed for this program.

Javits Gifted and Talented Education (2008 level: $7.5 million) supports activities to help high schools meet the educational needs of gifted and talented students. Current grants are not structured to assess program effectiveness and identify successful intervention strategies that could have broad national impact.

Education for Native Hawaiians (2008 level: $33.3 million) supports the provision of supplemental education services to the Native Hawaiian population. School districts that wish to implement programs and services tailored to the educational and cultural needs of Native Hawaiian students are able to use funds provided under other Federal programs. For example, significant funds are provided to Native Hawaiian students who receive services through Federal formula grant programs, such as Title I Grants to Local Educational Agencies and Special Education State Grants program.

Alaska Native Educational Equity (2008 level: $33.3 million) supports the provision of supplemental educational programs and services to Alaska Natives. The services provided to Alaska Native students through this program are redundant with many of those provided through the Department's Indian Education programs.

National Writing Project (2008 level: $23.6 million) provides a non-competitive grant to a nonprofit educational organization that promotes kindergarten through college level teacher training programs in writing. The 2006 PART assessment conducted by the Department of Education and OMB rated this program as Results Not Demonstrated. The program does not have data on its annual performance or long-term performance measures, and it lacks a rigorous evaluation of its effectiveness. Funds for training teachers in all academic subjects are provided under the Teacher Quality State Grants program.

School Leadership (2008 level: $14.5 million) supports recruiting, training, and retaining principals and assistant principals. The activities funded under this program can be funded under other authorities, including Teacher Quality State Grants.

Advanced Credentialing (2008 level: $9.6 million) supports the development of advanced credentials based on the content experience of master teachers. Funds also support related activities to encourage and support teachers seeking advanced credentials. Federal support for this program is no longer needed because the development and implementation of advanced credentialing systems through the National Board for Professional Teaching Standards and the American Board for the Certification of Teacher Excellence is complete. In addition, the Administration does not believe that additional funding for outreach, recruitment, or candidate subsidies is warranted without conclusive evidence that advancing credentialing increases student achievement.

Close-Up Fellowships (2008 level: $1.9 million) provides a non-competitive grant to the Close-Up Foundation to provide fellowships to low-income students and their teachers to finance their participation in one-week Washington, D.C. seminar programs to learn about the Federal

Government. In 1997, the Congress requested that the Close-Up Foundation provide a plan to continue its fellowships without Federal funding. In the succeeding years, the foundation surpassed its private sector fundraising goals. Given the popularity of this program and its successful private fundraising, the Administration believes this program would continue without Federal support.

Academies for American History and Civics (2008 level: $1.9 million) supports intensive workshops for teachers and students in the areas of history and civics. The activities funded under this program can be funded under other authorities, including Teacher Quality State Grants and Teaching American History.

Reading is Fundamental (2008 level: $24.6 million) awards an annual contract to the nonprofit literacy organization Reading is Fundamental, Inc. to provide aid to local nonprofit groups and volunteer organizations that serve low-income children through book distribution and reading motivation activities. These funds are required by statute to be awarded to a specific organization, rather than awarded under a competitive, merit-based process.

Ready to Teach (2008 level: $10.7 million) supports competitive grants to nonprofit telecommunications entities to carry out programs to improve teaching in core curriculum areas and to develop and distribute innovative educational and instructional video programming. Federal resources for these purposes are already available through the larger Teacher Quality State Grants program.

Exchanges with Historic Whaling and Trading Partners (2008 level: $8.8 million) provides non-competitive grants to support culturally based educational activities for Alaska Natives, Native Hawaiians, children and families of Massachusetts, and (as amended by Public Law 109-149) any federally-recognized Indian tribe in Mississippi. This program does not serve a national need, and could be best supported with State, local, and private funding.

Excellence in Economic Education (2008 level: $1.4 million) supports a competitive grant to a single nonprofit educational organization to promote economic and financial literacy for kindergarten through 12th grade (K-12) students. The activities funded under this program can be funded under other authorities and private sector outreach.

Mental Health Integration in Schools (2008 level: $4.9 million), first funded in 2005, provides grants to States and school districts to support collaborative efforts between school systems and mental health systems. The activities funded under this program can be funded under other authorities, including the Safe Schools/Healthy Students initiative within Safe and Drug-Free Schools National Programs.

Foundations for Learning (2008 level: $1.0 million), first funded in 2003, provides grants for comprehensive services to help children under seven who have multiple at-risk characteristics – including exposure to violence or abuse, low birth weight, and cognitive deficits – be prepared to enter school. A separate $1 million program for this purpose is not necessary, since Federal funding provided under IDEA, Head Start, and Title I all help at-risk preschool children enter school ready to learn.

Arts in Education (2008 level: $37.5 million) makes non-competitive awards to both VSA Arts and the John F. Kennedy Center for the Performing Arts, as well as competitive awards for demonstration projects and leadership activities to encourage the integration of arts into the school curriculum. School districts that are implementing arts education activities can use funds provided under other Federal programs for this purpose. Further, the Kennedy Center and VSA Arts have a long history of obtaining financial support from the private sector, individual donors, and other non-Federal sources. This financial support can be expected to continue even without this program.

Parental Information and Resource Centers (2008 level: $38.9 million) provide training, information, and support to State and local educational agencies and other organizations that carry out parent education and family involvement programs. Since parent education and support activities are required and funded under other No Child Left Behind programs such as Title I, a separate program for this purpose is not necessary.

Women's Educational Equity (2008 level: $1.8 million) supports activities promoting educational equity of girls and women. Since the enactment of the Women's Educational Equity Act in 1974, the need for a program focused on eliminating the educational gap for girls and women has diminished greatly, as women have made educational gains that match or exceed those of their male peers.

Alcohol Abuse Reduction (2008 level: $32.4 million) supports programs to reduce alcohol abuse in secondary schools. These activities are already supported by two activities the Budget funds within Safe and Drug-Free Schools National Programs – the $78 million Safe Schools/Healthy Students initiative, and the $10 million that is dedicated to research-based alcohol and drug use and violence prevention programs.

Mentoring (2008 level: $48.5 million) supports mentoring programs and activities for children who are at risk of educational failure, dropping out of school, involvement in criminal or delinquent activities, or who lack strong, positive role models. Mentoring activities are supported by many other Federal programs – the White House Task Force on Disadvantaged Youth identified over 100 youth programs which support mentoring in 13 agencies.

Elementary and Secondary School Counseling (2008 level: $48.6 million) makes grants to support elementary and secondary school counseling programs. Current statute requires that all appropriations below $40 million must be used for elementary school counseling. School counselors are primarily supported with non-Federal funds, and a small Federal categorical program can have, at best, a marginal impact on the number of counselors employed in schools or the availability of counseling for students, and has even less of an impact on the quality of the counseling provided. In addition, the Budget request for Safe and Drug Free Schools National Programs includes $78 million for the Safe Schools/Healthy Students initiative and $10 million dedicated to research-based alcohol and drug use and violence prevention programs – both of which districts may use to fund counseling as part of a comprehensive, research-based focus on the school environment.

Physical Education (2008 level: $75.7 million) supports physical education programs (including after-school programs) for students in K-12. The Department of Education and OMB assessed the program in 2005 using the PART and the program received a rating of Results Not Demonstrated. Physical Education programs have historically been supported by States and LEAs.

Civic Education (2008 level: $31.9 million) supports several non-competitive grants to organizations that promote civic responsibility through teacher training and instructional materials, and educational exchanges with developing democracies. Given the popularity of this program and its successful private fundraising, the Administration believes this program would continue without Federal support.

Department of Education: Discretionary Proposal
Small Postsecondary Student Financial Assistance Programs

Funding Summary
(In millions of dollars)

	2008 Level	2009 Proposed	Change From 2008
Budget Authority........................	172	---	-172

Administration Proposal and Impact

In 2009, the Budget proposes to terminate five small postsecondary student financial assistance programs totaling $172 million because they have either achieved their purpose or are duplicative of nearly $95 billion in grants, loans, and work study made available by the Department of Education each year. The Budget's proposals help address the findings and recommendations of the Secretary's Commission on the Future of Higher Education, which called for increasing need-based grant aid and simplifying the student aid programs.

These terminations are more than offset by the proposal in the 2009 Budget to increase the discretionary Pell Grant program by $2.6 billion. This increase, along with the $2 billion in mandatory funding provided under the College Cost Reduction and Access Act, will allow the maximum Pell Grant award to rise to $4,800 in 2009 and up to $5,400 by 2012. Overall the Budget will increase the amount of aid available to students, including a net $1.8 billion discretionary increase in need-based grant aid.

Background

The following five programs provide financial assistance to selected groups of postsecondary students. These programs have either served their mission or are duplicative of other Federal, State, local, or nonprofit activities.

Leveraging Educational Assistance Program (LEAP) (2008 level: $63.9 million) has accomplished its original objective of stimulating all States to establish need-based postsecondary student grant programs. However, beyond the establishment of these programs, LEAP does little to encourage States to increase their investment in grant aid for their neediest students, or effectively target this aid to the students who could most benefit from it. In 2004 the Department of Education and OMB assessed the program using the Program Assessment Rating Tool (PART) and rated it Results Not Demonstrated. The PART assessment also identified structural problems with LEAP that limited the program's effectiveness.

Perkins Loan Cancellations (2008 level: $64.3 million) provide loan forgiveness to certain Perkins Loan borrowers in exchange for undertaking certain public service employment, such as teaching in Head Start programs, full-time law enforcement, or nursing. In 2008, the $64.3 million Federal appropriation reimburses institutional revolving funds for these loan cancellations. The PART analysis conducted in 2004 rated the Perkins Loan program as Ineffective. It found that this program is duplicative of the direct and guaranteed student loan programs and is not well targeted to the neediest students. Eligible Perkins loans would continue to be cancelled but no appropriations would be made to replenish the institutional revolving funds. This program termination is coupled with the Budget's proposal to eliminate the Perkins loan program and recall the Federal portion of these revolving funds.

Byrd Scholarships (2008 level: $40.3 million) are intended to promote academic excellence through grants to States that support scholarship assistance for up to four years to high-performing high school students entering an undergraduate course of study. The program received a PART rating of Results Not Demonstrated because it lacks performance data and does not have a need-based component unlike other Department of Education postsecondary aid programs.

Thurgood Marshall Legal Educational Opportunity (2008 level: $2.9 million) provides minority, low-income, or disadvantaged college students with information, preparation, and financial assistance to help them gain access to and complete law school. This program is largely duplicative of similar assistance that is available through the Department's traditional postsecondary student financial aid programs.

B.J. Stupak Olympic Scholarships (2008 level: $1.0 million) provide financial assistance to athletes who are training at Olympic Training centers and who are pursuing a postsecondary education. This program lacks performance data to show progress toward meeting its goals and therefore received a PART rating of Results Not Demonstrated in 2004. Even with this termination, athletes may still receive grant, work-study, and loan assistance based on their financial need through the Department of Education's other postsecondary student aid programs.

Department of Education: Discretionary Proposal
Career and Technical Education State Grants and National Programs

Funding Summary
(In millions of dollars)

	2008 Level	2009 Proposed	Change From 2008
Budget Authority......................	1,169	---	-1,169

Administration Proposal and Impact

The Budget proposes to terminate the Career and Technical Education (CTE) State Grants program (formerly known as the Vocational Education State Grants program). The Administration believes the goals of this program could be better accomplished through the high school reforms included in the Administration's reauthorization proposal for No Child Left Behind. These reforms, in addition to the Budget's $406 million increase for Title I, will help improve academic achievement and graduation rates for at-risk high school students – many of whom are CTE students. The Administration's No Child Left Behind reauthorization proposal will also seek to close the achievement gap in middle and high schools through high standards and accountability, and to increase the rigor of coursework offered to middle and high school students to better prepare them for postsecondary education or the workforce.

Background

The CTE State Grants program provides grants to States to support high school and community college activities related to vocational and technical education. About two-thirds of the funding supports high school activities and the remainder supports postsecondary technical training. In its 2004 Final Report to the Congress, the National Assessment of Vocational Education found no evidence that high school vocational courses themselves contribute to academic achievement or college enrollment. The Department of Education and the Office of Management and Budget assessed the program using the Program Assessment Rating Tool (PART) in 2002. The PART rated Vocational Education State Grants as Ineffective because the program produced little evidence of improved outcomes for students despite decades of Federal investment. The Congress reauthorized the CTE program in 2006. While the CTE reauthorization added some new accountability measures, the Congress largely rejected the Administration's attempts to reform the program. This program, as a result, shows little promise of improving its record on student achievement.

Department of Education: Discretionary Proposal
Educational Technology State Grants

Funding Summary
(In millions of dollars)

	2008 Level	2009 Proposed	Change From 2008
Budget Authority.........................	267	---	-267

Administration Proposal and Impact

The Budget proposes to terminate the Educational Technology State Grants program and redirect its funding to higher priority programs that are more closely focused on student achievement and have a more rigorous accountability structure in place.

Background

The Educational Technology State Grants program supports funding for States and local school districts to utilize technology to improve instruction and student learning. It was created in the No Child Left Behind Act of 2001 as a consolidation of disparate educational technology programs. Funding supports teacher training in educational technology, technology deployment, and a host of other activities designed to utilize educational technology to improve student achievement.

While the program was created to better focus educational technology investments on student achievement, it is not clear that Educational Technology State Grants has been successful in accomplishing this mission. When the Department of Education and OMB recently completed a Program Assessment Rating Tool assessment of this program, they found that there are not yet enough data available to determine the program's impact on improving student academic achievement.

Educational technology may have a positive impact on student achievement, but it is not necessary to have a stand-alone Federal program solely dedicated to this purpose. States can continue to support similar activities through other, larger Department of Education programs, such as Title I Grants to Local Educational Agencies ($14.3 billion) and Teacher Quality State Grants ($2.8 billion).

The Congress decreased funding for this program from $496 million in 2005 to $272 million in 2006, a 45-percent decrease. The Congress further reduced funding to $267 million in 2008.

Department of Education: Discretionary Proposal
Even Start

Funding Summary
(In millions of dollars)

	2008 Level	2009 Proposed	Change From 2008
Budget Authority.........................	66	---	-66

Administration Proposal and Impact

In 2009, the Budget proposes to eliminate the Even Start program and redirect funds to programs that are likely to be more effective at improving early childhood education, including Title I. The 2002 Program Assessment Rating Tool (PART) assessment by the Department of Education and OMB, which rated Even Start as Ineffective due to its poor results on national evaluations over a number of years, provides strong justification for terminating the program.

Background

Launched as a small demonstration program in 1988, Even Start combines early childhood education, adult education, and parenting classes into "family literacy" programs for low-income children and their parents. However, three national evaluations of the program, including two with rigorous random control trial designs, show that Even Start is not effective. The children and adults who participate in the program do not make greater literacy gains than non-participants. The most recent evaluation concluded that, while Even Start participants made small gains, they did not perform better than the comparison group that did not receive Even Start services. In addition, the scores of Even Start participants after one year of participation in the program were very low. For example, Even Start children scored at the sixth percentile when tested at the end of the program on a measure of vocabulary knowledge and Even Start parents scored at the third grade level when tested at the end of the program on a measure of reading comprehension. Consequently, Even Start received an Ineffective PART rating in 2002.

In 2004, the Administration proposed to fund only continuation awards, based on PART findings and the national evaluations, and to begin phasing out the program. In 2005, the Administration proposed termination. The Congress provided the first funding reduction for the program in 2005 (-$22 million), reducing it from $247 million to $225 million. The Congress reduced the program further in 2006 to $99 million and in 2008 to $66 million.

Department of Education: Discretionary Proposal
Small Higher Education Programs

Funding Summary
(In millions of dollars)

	2008 Level	2009 Proposed	Change From 2008
Budget Authority.........................	30	---	-30

Administration Proposal and Impact

The Budget proposes to terminate funding for five small higher education grant programs because they support activities that may be carried out under other Department of Education programs, or have accomplished their intended missions and no longer require Federal support.

Background

The five programs discussed below provide support to certain postsecondary institutions for highly specialized purposes. These programs have either served their mission, do not have a significant national impact, or are duplicative of existing programs.

Strengthening Alaska Native and Native Hawaiian-serving Institutions (2008 level: $11.6 million) supports Alaska Native and Native Hawaiian-serving Institutions to enable them to improve and expand their capacity to serve Alaska Native and Native Hawaiian students. The types of activities supported by this program may be carried out under the Higher Education Act's Title III Strengthening Institutions program. Also, in both 2008 and 2009 this program will receive $15 million in mandatory funds provided by the College Cost Reduction and Access Act.

Tribally Controlled Postsecondary Career and Technical Institutions (2008 level: $7.5 million) provides grants to tribally controlled postsecondary career and technical institutions to provide career and technical education to Indian students. The statutory language for this program is written to limit eligibility to two institutions: United Tribes Technical College (Bismarck, ND) and Navajo Technical College (Crownpoint, NM). Even with this termination, these institutions would be eligible to apply for competitive grants under other Federal programs, including the Higher Education Act's Title III Strengthening Institutions program and the Strengthening Tribally Controlled Colleges and Universities program. The latter program is supported with mandatory funding in 2008 and 2009 under the College Cost Reduction and Access Act of 2007.

Demonstration Projects to Ensure Quality Higher Education for Students with Disabilities (2008 level: $6.8 million) funds technical assistance and professional development activities for faculty and administrators in institutions of higher education in order to improve the quality of education for students with disabilities. This program has achieved its primary goal of funding model demonstration projects. Similar projects can and do receive funding under the Fund for the Improvement of Postsecondary Education and programs within the Office of Special Education and Rehabilitation Services.

Underground Railroad (2008 level: $1.9 million) provides grants to nonprofit educational organizations to establish facilities that house, display, and interpret artifacts relating to the history of the Underground Railroad, as well as to make the interpretive efforts available to institutions of higher education. This program was not intended to provide a permanent source of funding, and prior grants have succeeded in spreading the history of the Underground Railroad through websites, expanded library collections, and private funding and endowment funds to support ongoing operations.

Teachers for a Competitive Tomorrow (2008 level: $2.0 million) provides competitive grants to partnerships to develop either baccalaureate or master's degree programs in science, technology, engineering, mathematics, or critical foreign languages that are integrated with teacher education and result in teacher certification. The activities supported by this program can also be supported under other Department of Education programs, including the Improving Teacher Quality State Grants program, Transition to Teaching program, and Troops to Teachers. In addition, the program is duplicative of the National Science Foundation's Robert Noyce Scholarship program, with includes a specific focus on training math and science teachers.

Department of Education: Discretionary Proposal
Small Vocational Rehabilitation Programs

Funding Summary
(In millions of dollars)

	2008 Level	2009 Proposed	Change From 2008
Budget Authority..........................	53	---	-53

Administration Proposal and Impact

In 2009, the Budget proposes to terminate the small Vocational Rehabilitation (VR) Migrant and Seasonal Farmworkers (MSFW), Projects with Industry, and Supported Employment programs, since these programs serve the same populations and provide the same services as VR State Grants. In addition, the Budget proposes to terminate VR Recreational Programs because the activities are more appropriately supported by State, local, and private entities.

Background

The following programs provide life skills or job training services to individuals with disabilities. Most are duplicative of the $2.9 billion Vocational Rehabilitation (VR) State grant program.

Supported Employment (2008 level: $29.2 million) was created in 1986 to encourage VR agencies to provide supported employment services to individuals with significant disabilities. At the time, supported employment was a new practice to employ individuals who traditionally would not be employed in integrated settings. Today, VR agencies recognize and utilize supported employment practices as an effective strategy to help individuals with significant disabilities obtain jobs. The Supported Employment program has achieved its original purpose. The 2007 Program Assessment Rating Tool (PART) review rated this program as Results Not Demonstrated because the program lacked long-term measures and targets, and could not demonstrate improved efficiencies.

Projects with Industry (PWI) (2008 level: $19.2 million) help individuals with disabilities obtain employment and advance their career in the competitive labor market. PWI is duplicative of the VR State Grants program because both provide the same services to the same target populations.

VR Recreational Programs (2008 level: $2.5 million) supports projects that provide recreation and related activities for individuals with disabilities to aid in their employment, mobility, independence, socialization, and community integration. The program has limited impact, and State and local agencies and the private sector can more appropriately provide these services.

VR Migrant and Seasonal Farmworkers (MSFW) (2008 level: $2.2 million) supports rehabilitation services to migratory workers with disabilities. Originally established as a demonstration program in the mid-1970s, the program no longer needs to demonstrate the benefits of serving migratory workers. The much larger VR State grants program serves the same population. In 2006, a PART review rated MSFW as Results Not Demonstrated because the program lacked long-term measures and targets, credible performance information, strategic planning, and sufficient oversight.

Department of Education: Discretionary Proposal
Smaller Learning Communities

Funding Summary
(In millions of dollars)

	2008 Level	2009 Proposed	Change From 2008
Budget Authority......................	80	---	-80

Administration Proposal and Impact

In 2009, the Budget proposes to terminate the Smaller Learning Communities program because of its narrow focus and lack of evidence of effectiveness. The populations served and services provided under this program are duplicative of Title I Grants to Local Educational Agencies. In addition, the Administration's No Child Left Behind reauthorization proposal will more effectively target funds to high schools with the most need.

Background

The Smaller Learning Communities program makes competitive grants to support the creation or expansion of smaller learning communities in large high schools. In 2005, the Department of Education and OMB assessed the program using the Program Assessment Rating Tool (PART) and rated it as Results Not Demonstrated. The PART findings noted the lack of rigorous evaluation data about the effects of smaller schools on performance and called attention to the diminished need for a specific Federal program to support the creation of smaller learning communities.

Since 2000, non-Federal funds have become available through the Carnegie Corporation of New York and the Bill and Melinda Gates Foundation, among others, to support multiyear high school reform initiatives that focus, in part, on creating smaller learning communities. In addition, records on the 2006 competition indicate that the grant awards were sharply concentrated geographically, with local educational agencies in two States (California and Florida) receiving 29 percent of the available funds. Interest in the program thus appears to be narrowly concentrated.

Department of Education: Discretionary Proposal
Special Olympics

Funding Summary
(In millions of dollars)

	2008 Level	2009 Proposed	Change From 2008
Budget Authority..........................	12	---	-12

Administration Proposal and Impact

The Budget proposes to terminate the Special Olympics program because the award must be made non-competitively to a designated grantee and is not the best way of ensuring that public funds are used effectively. Also, many of the activities to be supported under this program, such as increasing the participation of individuals with disabilities in the Special Olympics, are not directly supportive of the Department of Education's mission, and are more appropriately supported with private funds.

This elimination is consistent with the Administration's policy of increasing resources for higher priority programs, such as the Special Education Grants to States program, and eliminating small categorical programs that have limited impact. In addition, the Special Olympics has a long history of receiving significant private support, and should continue to receive this support without this Federal funding. In fact, for the year ended December 31, 2006, Special Olympics received $36 million in direct mail contributions and another $36 million from individual and corporate contributions and sponsorships.

Background

The Special Olympics Sport and Empowerment Act of 2004 authorizes awards by the Secretaries of Education, State, and Health and Human Services to Special Olympics to support activities related to the Special Olympics in a number of areas. Awards made by the Secretary of Education are authorized for:

- Activities to promote the expansion of Special Olympics, including activities to increase the participation of individuals with intellectual disabilities within the United States; and

- The design and implementation of Special Olympics education programs, including character education and volunteer programs that support the purposes of the Special Olympics Sport and Empowerment Act of 2004, that can be integrated into classroom instruction and are consistent with academic content standards.

Department of Education: Discretionary Proposal
State Grants for Incarcerated Youth Offenders

Funding Summary
(In millions of dollars)

	2008 Level	2009 Proposed	Change From 2008
Budget Authority…......................	22	---	-22

Administration Proposal and Impact

The Budget proposes to terminate the State Grants for Incarcerated Youth Offenders program because it is small, narrow-purpose, and has not demonstrated results. While the program is intended to support laudable purposes, it has not been evaluated and does not have strong administrative mechanisms for holding grantees accountable for outcomes.

In addition, this program is largely duplicative of the Department of Labor's Reintegration of Ex-Offenders (REO) program, for which the Budget requests $40 million. The REO program offers a range of job training, housing, and mentoring services for juveniles and adults. For juvenile offenders, REO provides a greater focus on building basic literacy and numeracy skills and the completion of secondary education through alternative education pathways, leading to career opportunities through postsecondary credentialing programs or pre-apprenticeship and apprenticeship programs.

Background

The State Grants for Incarcerated Youth Offenders program provides formula grants to State correctional agencies intended to assist and encourage incarcerated youth to acquire functional literacy and life and job skills.

Department of Education: Discretionary Proposal
Supplemental Educational Opportunity Grants

Funding Summary
(In millions of dollars)

	2008 level	2009 Proposed	Change From 2008
Budget Authority..........................	757	---	-757

Administration Proposal and Impact

In 2009, the Budget proposes to terminate the poorly targeted Supplemental Educational Opportunity Grants (SEOG) program that is duplicative of the larger and more targeted Federal Pell Grant program.

This termination is more than offset by the 2009 Budget's $2.6 billion discretionary funding increase for the Pell Grant program. This increase, along with the $2 billion in mandatory funding provided under the College Cost Reduction and Access Act, will allow the maximum Pell Grant award to rise to $4,800 in 2009 and up to $5,400 by 2012. Overall, the President's Budget will increase the amount of aid available to students, including a net $1.8 billion discretionary increase in need-based grant aid.

Unlike SEOG, the Budget's significant increases for Pell Grants will be broadly available to all eligible students, regardless of the institution they attend.

Background

The Supplemental Educational Opportunity Grant (SEOG) program provides grant assistance to students through institutions of higher education, which provide 25 percent in matching funds. Only about seven percent of postsecondary students receive funding under SEOG, compared to the nearly one-quarter who receive Pell Grants. The amount of Federal matching funds provided to institutions varies widely and is determined by a statutory formula that benefits more established institutions. This antiquated allocation formula means that proportionately less SEOG funding goes to institutions that educate the largest proportion of low-income students. In 2006 for instance, while nearly 65 percent of Pell Grant recipients enrolled in public institutions of higher education, these institutions only received 45 percent of SEOG funds to provide to needy students.

Additionally, SEOG awards are not optimally allocated based on financial need. Though institutions are required by statute to give "priority" in awarding SEOG funds to Pell-eligible students, there is no requirement that the size of these awards be tied to a student's need, and institutions have discretion to provide larger SEOG awards to students without the highest need.

Compared to Pell Grants, a higher proportion of SEOG funds support administrative costs and a lower proportion goes to students at institutions of higher education. While only 0.1 percent of Pell Grant funding is available to institutions to pay for administrative costs, 5 percent of SEOG funding is used for this purpose.

In a 2003 Program Assessment Rating Tool review, SEOG was found to be duplicative of other programs, not effectively targeted, and unable to demonstrate results.

Department of Education: Discretionary Proposal
Teacher Quality Enhancement Program

Funding Summary
(In millions of dollars)

	2008 Enacted	2009 Proposed	Change From 2008
Budget Authority.........................	34	---	-34

Administration Proposal and Impact

The Budget proposes to eliminate funding for the Teacher Quality Enhancement program, as the program has failed to demonstrate results and many of its activities can be supported under a number of other programs within the Department of Education, including the $2.8 billion Improving Teacher Quality State Grants program. The Budget includes funding for other activities designed to improve teacher quality, including support for the Teacher Incentive Fund, Transition to Teaching, Troops to Teachers and an Adjunct Teacher Corps initiative to bring more qualified mid-career professionals into the classroom.

Background

The Teacher Quality Enhancement program, first funded in 1998, provides support for multiple types of activities, including Recruitment and Partnership Grants that support collaboration between schools of education and local school districts to recruit and train teachers to serve in high-need schools, and Grants to States for reforming their teacher preparation and accreditation systems.

In 2004, the Department of Education and OMB completed a Program Assessment Rating Tool (PART) evaluation of this program and gave it a rating of Results Not Demonstrated due to its lack of performance information. The PART assessment also noted that the program's authorizing statute specifies how funds must be allocated across program components, limiting the Department's ability to manage the program effectively. While in response to the PART assessment the program has developed long-term and annual performance measures and collected data for these measures, it has not produced evidence that it is improving the quality of teacher preparation programs. In addition, the program still lacks a rigorous evaluation that demonstrates its effectiveness.

The Congress has reduced funding for this program by $55 million over the prior four years, from $89 million in 2004 to $34 million in 2008.

Department of Education: Discretionary Proposal
Tech-Prep Education State Grants

Funding Summary
(In millions of dollars)

	2008 Level	2009 Proposed	Change From 2008
Budget Authority......................	103	---	-103

Administration Proposal and Impact

In 2009, the Budget proposes to terminate Tech-Prep State grants and redirect the funds to activities focused on strengthening high school education in general, rather than supporting this lower-priority, narrowly focused program. In addition, the Administration's No Child Left Behind reauthorization proposal will support linkages between secondary schools and postsecondary institutions.

Background

The Tech-Prep State Grants program supports partnerships that develop structural links between secondary schools and postsecondary institutions to integrate academic and vocational education. About two-thirds of the funds support high school activities. In 2002, the Department of Education and OMB assessed the program using the Program Assessment Rating Tool and found that the program could not demonstrate results based on a series of national evaluations indicating that the program provides no measurable advantage for high school students in terms of high school completion, postsecondary enrollment, and academic achievement.

Department of Energy: Discretionary Proposal
Oil and Gas Research and Development

Funding Summary
(In millions of dollars)

	2008 Enacted	2009 Proposed	Change From 2008
Budget Authority..........................	25	---	-25

Administration Proposal and Impact

The Budget provides for the orderly termination of the Oil and Gas Research and Development (R&D) programs. These R&D activities typically fund development of technologies that can be commercialized quickly, like improved drill motors. Therefore it is more appropriate for the oil and gas industry to perform these activities. In addition, the programs have not demonstrated results, as identified in the 2003 Program Assessment Rating Tool (PART) review and updated annually. The industry has both the financial incentives and resources to develop inexpensive and safe methods to extract oil and gas. The termination of the programs will be structured to avoid disruption to the Federal workforce, respecting existing contractual obligations and minimizing new contractual obligations in 2008 that would require activity in 2009.

Background

The Oil and Gas R&D programs develop technologies that industry can use to reduce the cost of exploration and production of oil and natural gas reserves. On April 25, 2006, President Bush stated, "…energy companies don't need unnecessary tax breaks like the write-offs of certain geological and geophysical expenditures, or the use of taxpayers' money to subsidize energy companies' research into deep water drilling."

The programs focus on incremental and evolutionary technology advances that oil and gas companies have the resources and incentives to conduct, which is not in accordance with the Administration's R&D Investment Criteria. PART analysis of program performance rated the Oil and Gas R&D programs Ineffective, largely on their failure to demonstrate clear results.

Nuclear Regulatory Commission: Discretionary Proposal
University Nuclear Energy Program

Funding Summary
(In millions of dollars)

	2008 Enacted	2009 Proposed	Change From 2008
Budget Authority........................	15	---	-15

Administration Proposal and Impact

The University Nuclear Energy Program assisted universities in maintaining research and education reactors, as well as providing dedicated fellowships for students studying nuclear engineering. This program has historically been located in the Department of Energy (DOE), but beginning in 2007, the Administration proposed termination. In 2008, the Congress moved responsibility for the education assistance activity to the Nuclear Regulatory Commission. The program initially came about in response to low enrollment. At this point, target levels for undergraduate enrollment have been met, and the number of universities offering nuclear-related programs also has increased. In addition, the Nuclear Regulatory Commission expects to receive from the nuclear industry approximately 20 combined construction and operating licenses for upward of 30 new nuclear power reactors. These trends reflect renewed interest in nuclear power. Universities, along with nuclear industry societies and utilities are expected to continue to invest in university research reactors, students, and faculty members and, therefore, students will continue to be drawn into this course of study. Consequently, federal assistance is no longer necessary, and the Budget proposes termination of this program. This termination is also supported by the fact that the program was unable to demonstrate results from its activities when reviewed using the Program Assessment Rating Tool. The Budget includes $3.7 million at DOE to continue supporting reactor fuel services for universities.

There are other more appropriate mechanisms to support nuclear education. For example, in 2009 through its Nuclear Energy Research Initiative, DOE's Office of Nuclear Energy will designate at least 20 percent of funds appropriated to its research and development programs for work to be performed at university and research institutions. This commitment to strengthening the Nation's nuclear education infrastructure directly supports the goals of the American Competes Act of 2007.

Background

The University Nuclear Energy Program was designed to address declining enrollment levels among U.S. nuclear engineering programs. Since the late 1990s, enrollment levels in nuclear education programs have tripled, although the University Nuclear Energy Program is not able to demonstrate that its actions are responsible for this increase. Additionally, the program projected that U.S. enrollment levels reaching upward of 1,500 students would be needed by the year 2015 – with enrollments having reached this level in 2005, there is no longer a need for this program.

Department of Energy: Discretionary Proposal
Weatherization Assistance Program

Funding Summary
(In millions of dollars)

	2008 Enacted	2009 Proposed	Change From 2008
Budget Authority........................	227[1]	---	-227

[1] In Table S-5, Discretionary Program Termination and Reductions, in the main *Budget* volume, 2008 Enacted for the Weatherization Assistance Program was reported incorrectly as $243 million. The correct figure, $227 million, is displayed above.

Administration Proposal and Impact

The Budget proposes to eliminate funding for the Weatherization Assistance Program and redirect the funding to higher priority Department of Energy (DOE) R&D efforts. These programs will yield long term benefits to all Americans. Using these funds to support the President's Advanced Energy Initiative (AEI) and energy efficiency efforts will save energy and help accelerate development of clean energy sources that can transform the way America powers its homes, businesses, and vehicles, and can help reduce the Nation's dependence on oil.

Financial assistance for energy efficiency upgrades is not in line with DOE's core mission or goals. In addition, the return on investment of the Weatherization Assistance Program is significantly less than some alternative uses of these funds. DOE estimates that the Weatherization program has a benefit-cost ratio of about 1.5 to 1.0. For comparison, the Department estimates that the historical return on its energy efficiency portfolio is about 20 to 1.

There are other sources of funding for weatherization activities. The Low Income Home Energy Assistance Program (LIHEAP) in the Department of Health and Human Services allows some of its funds to be used for weatherization assistance. States also provide non-Federal low-income energy assistance, mostly in the form of credits and discounts from utilities companies. In 2006, 38 States reported almost $2.7 billion in non-Federal low-income energy assistance.

Background

The Weatherization Assistance Program provides formula grants to States to improve the home energy efficiency (e.g., by insulating walls and attics) of low-income families, thus reducing their energy bills. LIHEAP allows States to use up to 15 percent of the grant they receive for weatherization assistance.

The 2002 Budget proposed to significantly increase funding for this program, resulting in an increase in appropriations of more than $75 million in 2002 to $230 million. The Congress provided similar funding levels through 2008. Beginning with the 2007 Budget, the Administration has refocused these resources on the President's AEI and other investments. The Budget redirects the funding to renewable energy programs within AEI, and to programs that focus on energy efficiency improvements.

Department of Health and Human Services: Discretionary Proposal
Community Services Block Grant (CSBG)

Funding Summary
(In millions of dollars)

	2008 Enacted	2009 Proposed	Change From 2008
Budget Authority..........................	654	---	-654

Administration Proposal and Impact

The Budget proposes to terminate the Community Services Block Grant (CSBG) because it lacks appropriate performance measures and lacks competition as evidenced by the same grantees receiving funding year after year. For example, over 1,000 Community Action Agencies (CAAs) that receive CSBG funding have little incentive to improve their performance since they are not held to minimum performance standards as a condition for continued grant awards. The average grantee does not rely on CSBG as its primary funding source; CSBG dollars make up less than 10 percent of the average grantee's budget. The Budget also proposes to terminate CSBG because key services provided with program dollars are duplicative of other Federal programs benefiting low-income populations. Further, these other Federal programs are larger and may better address the needs of the poor by focusing resources on a specific service instead of providing for a wide range of services with diffuse CSBG funding.

Background

CSBG was created in 1981 to reduce poverty, revitalize low-income communities and empower low-income families and individuals to be self-sufficient. This flexible funding reaches almost every county in the Nation through State-administered networks of local Community Action Agencies (CAAs) to promote activities that reduce the incidence and severity of poverty. Services categories include employment, education, housing, nutrition, income management, and health, which are targeted to low-income individuals with a special focus on Temporary Assistance to Needy Families enrollees, the homeless, migrant farm workers, and low-income elderly. The program does not have appropriate performance measures and has a program purpose that is too broad and duplicative of other anti-poverty programs.

Department of Health and Human Services: Discretionary Proposal
ACF Other Community Service Programs

Funding Summary
(In millions of dollars)

	2008 Enacted	2009 Proposed	Change From 2008
Budget Authority..	45	---	-45
Community Economic Development	32	---	-32
Rural Community Facilities	8	---	-8
Job Opportunities for Low-Income Individuals.	5	---	-5

Administration Proposal and Impact

The Budget proposes to eliminate three community services programs: 1) Community Economic Development; 2) Rural Community Facilities; and 3) Job Opportunities for Low-Income Individuals. These programs do not have performance standards to assess their impact, are too narrowly focused to have a major benefit, duplicate other Federal programs, and award grants on a noncompetitive basis. The Budget focuses resources on other, higher priority programs.

Background

The *Community Economic Development* program was created in 1981 to award grants to private and nonprofit organizations to create new employment and business opportunities for low-income individuals. Projects include business start-ups, expansions, development of new products and services, and other physical and commercial improvements. The targeted population includes the unemployed, public assistance recipients, residents of public housing, the homeless, and individuals transitioning from incarceration into the community. The program also duplicates the efforts of existing Federal programs such as Temporary Assistance for Needy Families. Thirty-six grants were awarded with $27 million in 2007.

The *Rural Community Facilities* program, created in 1981, awards grants to nonprofits, State, and local governments to develop affordable, safe water and waste water treatment facilities. Funding is used to provide training and technical assistance in developing and managing water facilities; improve coordination of Federal, State and local agencies with waste and water management; and distribute information to local communities on available Federal resources. The program is duplicative of other Federal entities such as the Bureau of Reclamation's Rural Water Program, which is responsible for water and waste water treatment facilities. Eight grants were awarded with $7 million in 2007.

The *Job Opportunities for Low-Income Individuals* program was authorized in 1988 to award grants to nonprofit organizations to create new full-time, permanent employment opportunities for low-income individuals. Examples of job creation projects include expansion of existing businesses, and self-employment/micro-enterprises. Local communities may provide similar services targeted to low-income individuals with funding from the Community Development Block Grant program in the Department of Commerce. Eleven grants were awarded with $5 million in 2007.

Department of Health and Human Services: Discretionary Proposal
Alzheimer's Demonstration Projects

Funding Summary
(In millions of dollars)

	2008 Enacted	2009 Proposed	Change From 2008
Budget Authority…......................	11	---	-11

Administration Proposal and Impact

The Budget proposes to eliminate the Alzheimer's Demonstration Projects. Over the past 15 years, this program has provided grants to all States to seek out innovative practices in caring for people with Alzheimer's disease. Program dollars can now be better spent on disseminating information on successful, replicable, and innovative Alzheimer's care programs.

Background

The Alzheimer's Demonstration Projects program provides grants to States to develop innovative approaches in caring for individuals with Alzheimer's disease and supporting families and caregivers of Alzheimer's patients. Examples of previously supported innovations include increasing awareness of dementia in African-American communities through local churches; providing a safe and stimulating environment for Alzheimer's patients in adult care; and targeting low-income, rural, and ethnic communities through local outreach. Since the demonstration project was first created in 1992, all States have received funding. Also, of the 38 States that received funding in 2005, all are former grantees with a quarter of these States having received funding since 1992.

Department of Health and Human Services: Discretionary Proposal
Preventive Health Services

Funding Summary
(In millions of dollars)

	2008 Enacted	2009 Proposed	Change From 2008
Budget Authority..........................	21	---	-21

Administration Proposal and Impact

The Budget proposes to terminate the Administration on Aging's (AOA's) Preventive Health Services program because it is duplicative of services that States can provide through AOA's Community-Based Supportive Services program. Also, AOA envisions integrating prevention as an underlying principle in its core programs and advocating use of evidence-based programs to better address preventive health needs versus the current mechanism of providing a small funding stream of unfocused seed money through the Preventive Health Services program.

Background

The Preventive Health Services program supports activities that educate and promote healthy behavior that can help to prevent or delay chronic disease and disability among older Americans. Examples of activities that take place in multi-purpose senior center and other community-based settings include medication management classes; alcohol and substance abuse prevention and smoking cessation programs; physical fitness classes; and health screenings and risk assessments for conditions such as hypertension, diabetes, cholesterol, hearing, vision, and glaucoma. All of these services can be supported by AOA's Community-Based Supportive Services program.

Department of Health and Human Services: Discretionary Proposal
Preventive Health and Health Services Block Grant

Funding Summary
(In millions of dollars)

	2008 Enacted	2009 Proposed	Change From 2008
Budget Authority............................	97	---	-97

Administration Proposal and Impact

The Budget proposes no funding for the Centers for Disease Control and Prevention (CDC) Preventive Health and Health Services Block Grant (PHHSBG). The Budget continues to make substantial investments in the public health system through State and local bioterrorism preparedness grants and other categorical public health grants to States.

Background

PHHSBG was authorized in 1981 through the consolidation of multiple categorical programs. PHHSBG activities focus on chronic disease prevention, public health infrastructure, access to healthcare, injury reduction, prevention and services for sex offenses, immunizations and infectious diseases, and other activities. In 2007, the average award to States/Territories was approximately $2 million.

PHHSBG lacks national level performance outcome information and overlaps with categorical funding. The block grant was created through the consolidation of multiple categorical grants. Since the establishment of PHHSBG, categorical grants have reemerged that cover many of the same areas. In the main areas covered by the block grant, CDC categorical programs have grown to more than $800 million a year.

Department of Health and Human Services: Discretionary Proposal
Congressional Earmarks

Funding Summary
(In millions of dollars)

	2008 Enacted	2009 Proposed	Change From 2008
Food and Drug Administration......	5	---	-5
Health Resources and Services Administration........................	368	---	-368
Centers for Disease Control and Prevention.............................	27	---	-27
Substance Abuse and Mental Health Services Administration.....	19	---	-19
Centers for Medicare and Medicaid Services................................	5	---	-5
Administration on Aging............	6	---	-6
Administration for Children and Families................................	17	---	-17
General Departmental Management..........................	4	---	-4
Total, Budget Authority...............	**451**	**---**	**-451**

Administration Proposal and Impact

The Budget does not fund $451 million for over 1,200 activities that are earmarked to specific projects and recipients in the Consolidated Appropriations Act 2008. These earmarks, which are not awarded through the merit-based or competitive process, do not represent the most effective use of Federal dollars. Examples include funds to employ a counselor and pay for retreats for Wisconsin farmers and facilities construction. The Budget proposes that such funding be redirected to other activities that can be targeted toward high priorities through a competitive grant process.

Background

The Budget requests no funding for the congressional earmarks to specific projects and recipients. These earmarks divert funding from other higher priority programs, circumvent competitive processes, and divert people and associated financial resources from the Agency's core mission activities.

Department of Health and Human Services: Discretionary Proposal
Children's Hospital Graduate Medical Education Payment Program

Funding Summary
(In millions of dollars)

	2008 Enacted	2009 Proposed	Change From 2008
Budget Authority......................	302	---	-302

Administration Proposal and Impact

The Budget proposes to eliminate funding for the Children's Hospital Graduate Medical Education Payment Program. These payments do not purchase services, but represent a general financial subsidy to children's hospitals that can be used for any purpose. In addition, children's hospitals receive some payments from other public and private sources. A Program Assessment Rating Tool (PART) evaluation conducted by the Department of Health and Human Services and OMB concluded there is not a demonstrated need for this formula-driven subsidy as children's hospitals are more likely to have positive profit margins than other hospitals.

Background

The Children's Hospitals Graduate Medical Education Payment Program (which began in 2000 and was initially funded at $40 million) finances payments to free-standing children's hospitals that support graduate medical education. This payment activity was created because these hospitals receive little or no Medicare Graduate Medical Education funding. These payments are provided via a statutory formula that incorporates the number of residents, number of discharges, number of beds, and the hospital's case-mix.

The Administration proposed reduced funding for this activity in the 2006, 2007, and 2008 Budgets. In 2007, the Congress reauthorized this activity without significant reform at $330 million annually.

Department of Health and Human Services: Discretionary Proposal
Maternal and Child Health Small Categorical Grants

Funding Summary
(In millions of dollars)

	2008 Enacted	2009 Proposed	Change From 2008
Budget Authority….....................	40	---	-40

Administration Proposal and Impact

The Budget proposes no funding for Health Resources and Services Administration's (HRSA) Maternal and Child Health small categorical grants (Universal Newborn Hearing Screening, Traumatic Brain Injury, and Emergency Medical Services for Children). In 2004, the Traumatic Brain Injury and Emergency Medical Services programs both received ratings of Results not Demonstrated when the Department of Health and Human Services and OMB assessed them using the Program Assessment Rating Tool (PART). A 2005 PART evaluation of the Universal Newborn Hearing Screening Program determined that the program had completed its intended objective of helping States to implement universal newborn hearing screening.

Background

The activities funded by these small grant programs can continue to be conducted by States through their Maternal and Child Health Block Grant and other sources. The Maternal and Child Health Block Grant at HRSA allocates $666 million to States to fund activities for mothers, children, and their families.

Department of Health and Human Services: Discretionary Proposal
Urban Indian Health Program

Funding Summary
(In millions of dollars)

	2008 Enacted	2009 Proposed	Change From 2008
Budget Authority…........................	35	---	-35

Administration Proposal and Impact

The Budget proposes to phase out Urban Indian Health funding and target funds to health care services to American Indians and Alaska Natives living on or near reservations. It is expected that some Urban Indian Clinics will continue to deliver services using funding from other sources. American Indians and Alaska Natives residing in urban areas will have access to health care services through other public and private health insurance and other sources of care.

Background

The Urban Indian Health Program, established in 1976, finances grants and contracts for primary, preventive, and behavioral health care, as well as outreach and referral services, for the 60 percent of American Indians and Alaska Natives that live in urban areas. A Program Assessment Rating Tool (PART) assessment conducted by the Department of Health and Human Services and OMB rated the program Adequate but identified flaws, such as the lack of independent evaluations of service delivery and effectiveness. Approximately 60 percent of the operating budgets for providers that receive Urban Indian Health funding come from other public and private sources. Unlike many American Indians and Alaska Natives who live in rural areas and on reservations, urban Indians can readily access publicly and privately financed health care services.

Department of Housing and Urban Development: Discretionary Proposal
Brownfields Economic Development Initiative Program

Funding Summary
(In millions of dollars)

	2008 Enacted	2009 Proposed	Change From 2008
Budget Authority............................	10	---	-10

Administration Proposal and Impact

The Budget proposes to terminate the Department of Housing and Urban Development's Brownfields Economic Development Initiative (BEDI) program. BEDI is duplicative as its activities can be funded with Community Development Block Grant (CDBG) funds. Further, the program has performance deficiencies that include slow expenditure of funding and lengthy time frames to produce tangible results.

Background

BEDI is a competitive grant program designed to assist cities start redevelopment or continue phased redevelopment efforts on Brownfields sites where either potential or actual environmental conditions are known and redevelopment plans exist. The purpose of these activities is to return Brownfields to productive economic use. Brownfields are abandoned, idled, and underused industrial and commercial facilities and land where expansion and redevelopment is burdened by real or potential environmental contamination. BEDI grants must be used in conjunction with a new Section 108-guaranteed loan commitment from HUD.

In 2004, a crosscutting review of Federal community and economic development programs found that many of these programs, including BEDI, had unclear objectives, did not coordinate effectively, were duplicative, and were unable to demonstrate measurable and sustained economic gains for communities.

Department of Housing and Urban Development: Discretionary Proposal
HOPE VI

Funding Summary
(In millions of dollars)

	2008 Enacted	2009 Proposed	Change From 2008
Budget Authority….....................	100	---	-100

Administration Proposal and Impact

The Budget proposes to terminate the Revitalization of Severely Distressed Public Housing (HOPE VI) program. The program has surpassed it primary goal to demolish 100,000 severely distressed public housing units. While the program has achieved success in removing substandard public housing, the 2005 Program Assessment Rating Tool (PART) analysis and a Government Accountability Office (GAO) report showed the program to be slow at completing construction and more costly than other programs that serve the same population. The Budget includes funding increases for more cost-effective alternatives, such as the HOME block grant and Section 8 Tenant-based Assistance.

Background

In 1992, the Congress established the HOPE VI program to address 100,000 of the most severely distressed public housing units in the Nation's urban neighborhoods by 2003. Through competitive grants, HOPE VI has awarded local public housing authorities over $6 billion to demolish, rehabilitate, and replace obsolete public housing with mixed-income communities, as well as provide social services to residents.

The program was originally designed with a discrete target – demolish 100,000 substandard public housing units by the end of 2003. Today, that goal has been exceeded by more than 50,000 units and additional units will be demolished and replaced with less dense units as the program's $1.4 billion in balances are expended over the next several years. GAO found the housing-related costs of a HOPE VI unit were more than 25-percent higher than a housing voucher and more than 40-percent higher when non-housing costs were included. The program has been slow to produce results; typically seven years pass between the time a HOPE VI award is made and when the new units are occupied. In contrast, other Federal programs, such as HOME block grants, produce new housing units more expeditiously and cost-effectively. Given that the program has exceeded its primary objective, has higher per-unit costs than other alternatives, and has had extensive delays, HOPE VI should be terminated.

Department of Housing and Urban Development: Discretionary Proposal
Rural Housing and Economic Development

Funding Summary
(In millions of dollars)

	2008 Enacted	2009 Proposed	Change From 2008
Budget Authority..........................	17	---	-17

Administration Proposal and Impact

The Budget proposes to terminate the Rural Housing and Economic Development (RHED) Program in the Department of Housing and Urban Development (HUD). RHED is duplicative, particularly with programs provided through the Department of Agriculture, which manages a portfolio of rural housing and economic development grant programs that vastly exceeds HUD's RHED in terms of services, budget, loan, staffing, and expertise.

Background

RHED was first authorized in 1989 to encourage different approaches to serve the housing and economic development needs of the Nation's rural communities. In 2004, the Administration's crosscutting review of Federal community and economic development programs found that many of these programs, including RHED, had unclear objectives, did not coordinate effectively, were duplicative, and were unable to demonstrate measurable and sustained economic gains for communities. The Program Assessment Rating Tool (PART) assessment conducted by HUD and OMB rated RHED as Ineffective. Its major problems include its lack of annual and long-term outcome measures, duplicative mission, and inability to produce transparent information on results.

Department of Housing and Urban Development: Discretionary Proposal
Section 108 Community Development Loan Program

Funding Summary
(In millions of dollars)

	2008 Enacted	2009 Proposed	Change From 2008
Budget Authority.........................	5	---	-5

Administration Proposal and Impact

The Budget proposes to terminate the Department of Housing and Urban Development's Section 108 Community Development Loan Guarantee Program. Other programs and more attractive financing options are available to fund the program's projects and address its objectives. In addition, communities do not commonly utilize the loan program because they have to pledge their current and potential future Community Development Block Grant (CDBG) funds as the principal security for the loan guarantee, as well as any additional security that may be determined necessary.

Background

Section 108 is the loan guarantee provision of the CDBG program, which became an active program in 1979. The program offers communities a source of financing for economic development, housing rehabilitation, public facilities, and large-scale physical development projects. In 2004, a cross-cutting review of Federal community and economic development programs found that many of these programs, including the Section 108 Loan Guarantee Program, had unclear objectives, did not coordinate effectively, were duplicative, and were unable to demonstrate measurable and sustained economic gains for communities. This program received a Results Not Demonstrated on its 2006 Program Assessment Rating Tool.

Department of the Interior: Discretionary Proposal
Bureau of Indian Affairs' Housing Improvement Program

Funding Summary
(In millions of dollars)

	2008 Enacted	2009 Proposed	Change From 2008
Budget Authority......................	14	---	-14

Administration Proposal and Impact

The Budget proposes to terminate funding for the Bureau of Indian Affairs' Housing Improvement Program (HIP). A 2004 Program Assessment Rating Tool analysis found that the program was duplicative with, or served the same eligible population as, the Department of Housing and Urban Development's (HUD's) Native American Housing Assistance and Self-Determination Program, which is funded at approximately $700 million annually. HUD allows the Tribes to determine and address low-income housing needs through a block grant program. Often a Tribe requires recipients to repay some portion of the cost provided under the HUD program as a stipulation for receiving funding. The HIP program does not require recipients to repay; however, nothing in the law or HUD's regulations would prevent the Tribes from including these individuals under the HUD grant.

Background

The HIP program provides funding to eligible Tribes for renovations of existing homes or for construction of a house for tribal members who do not own a home but own sufficient land suitable for housing on or near a reservation. Funds are provided to the Tribes through grants. Applicants must go through a ranking process each year based on income, age, disability, and number of dependent children despite how they ranked the previous year, which can be administratively burdensome to the Tribes. The Congress did not eliminate the program in 2008; however, funding was decreased by $9.5 million, or -41 percent.

Department of the Interior: Discretionary Proposal
Bureau of Indian Education Johnson-O'Malley Assistance Grants

Funding Summary
(In millions of dollars)

	2008 Enacted	2009 Proposed	Change From 2008
Budget Authority.........................	21	---	-21

Administration Proposal and Impact

The Budget proposes to terminate funding for the Johnson-O'Malley Assistance Grants. The Bureau of Indian Education's (BIE's) core responsibility for education is to provide a basic program for approximately 44,000 Native American children attending BIE schools. The State public schools have other sources of funding for activities provided by the Johnson-O'Malley grants. These schools can apply for supplemental education funding from other State and Federal agencies – for example, from the Department of Education's Indian Education Grants to Local Education Agencies and Special Programs for Indian Children.

Background

Johnson-O'Malley grants are given to federally-recognized Tribes for the Tribes to distribute to local public elementary and secondary schools. About 93 percent of Native American children attend State public elementary and secondary schools across the Nation. This supplemental financial assistance to public schools has been provided for these schools to include culturally-related education for Indian students, as well as tutoring and counseling services.

Department of the Interior: Discretionary Proposal
Bureau of Indian Affairs' Indian Land Consolidation Program

Funding Summary
(In millions of dollars)

	2008 Enacted	2009 Proposed	Change From 2008
Budget Authority.....................	10	---	-10

Administration Proposal and Impact

The Budget proposes to eliminate funding for the Bureau of Indian Affairs' Indian Land Consolidation Program (ILCP), which purchases small, fractional interests in millions of acres of lands held in trust by the Federal Government on behalf of individual Indians. The program consolidates ownership of the lands to enable Tribes to effectively manage their lands and put them to productive use. In the past, the program's operating strategy has ranged from purchasing interests on a first-come/first-served basis from any willing seller to concentrating on tracts with 200 or more owners. The Administration is proposing to eliminate the program and work with the Congress and the Tribes to develop alternative approaches.

Background

There are some 3.6 million interests on over 128,000 tracts of land, totaling between 10 million and 13 million acres, held in trust by the Federal Government on behalf of more than 300,000 individual Indians. The Federal Government is responsible for maintaining the ownership title for each person (despite the size of the person's interest in the tract), negotiating and managing leases on the lands, and distributing any revenue. It costs tens of millions of dollars to track and manage these interests, which is not cost effective relative to the amount of income generated or the possibility of lawsuits, such as *Cobell vs. Kempthorne*. Since 1999, ILCP has spent nearly $170 million to purchase over 360,000 of these interests and consolidate about 400 tracts, yet this has done little to reduce trust management costs. A new approach is needed.

Department of the Interior: Discretionary Proposal
Land and Water Conservation Fund State Recreation Grants

Funding Summary
(In millions of dollars)

	2008 Enacted	2009 Proposed	Change From 2008
Budget Authority.........................	25	---	-25

Administration Proposal and Impact

The Budget proposes to terminate Land and Water Conservation Fund (LWCF) State discretionary recreation grants. These grants pay for improvements to State and local parks, which are decisions better left to State and local taxpayers than to Federal taxpayers. Federal funding for local parks and recreation programs is not a national priority.

In addition, a Program Assessment Rating Tool (PART) review found that this program had not been able to measure performance or demonstrate results.

Background

LWCF State recreation grants provide matching Federal funds for State and local governments to acquire lands or make improvements to State and local parks.

Annual funding for LWCF State recreation grants recently has ranged from zero in the late 1990s to $140 million in 2002. No funding has been requested in the past four years, partly because a 2003 PART review gave the program a low (25 percent) rating. LWCF State recreation grants are distinct from LWCF Federal land acquisition programs at the National Park Service, Fish and Wildlife Service, Bureau of Land Management, and the Department of Agriculture's Forest Service.

The Gulf of Mexico Energy Security Act (P.L. 109-432, Division C, Title I) allocates 12.5 percent of receipts from new oil and gas leases in the Gulf of Mexico to fund this program with mandatory funds. This mandatory funding could provide up to $10 million a year over the next few years and over $150 million a year in the out-years for LWCF State recreation grants.

Department of the Interior: Discretionary Proposal
National Park Service Statutory Aid

Funding Summary
(In millions of dollars)

	2008 Enacted	2009 Proposed	Change From 2008
Budget Authority..........................	7	---	-7

Administration Proposal and Impact

The Budget terminates National Park Service (NPS) "statutory aid" grants to various non-Federal entities that conduct historical or recreational activities, such as the Southwest Pennsylvania Heritage Preservation Commission and a Native Hawaiian Culture and Arts program. These activities are secondary to the NPS mission and are not a Federal responsibility. They also have no performance requirements and have not demonstrated results.

Background

The NPS statutory aid program consists of a variety of small congressional earmarks to various groups that have some connection to conservation, historic preservation, or outdoor recreation.

The Executive Branch historically has sought to limit the number of these grants, because they are not subject to a competitive merit-based process and generally do not fund national priorities. There are no performance requirements for this "pass-through" funding.

Starting with the 2005 Budget, the Administration has proposed to completely eliminate these grants in order to concentrate resources on higher Federal priorities, such as maintaining national parks. As a result, funding for statutory aid has dropped from $14 million in 2001 to $7 million in 2008.

Department of the Interior: Discretionary Proposal
Office of Surface Mining Coal Reclamation Grants

Funding Summary
(In millions of dollars)

	2008 Enacted	2009 Proposed	Change From 2008
Budget Authority.........................	20	---	-20

Administration Proposal and Impact

The Budget proposes to terminate the Office of Surface Mining's (OSM's) coal reclamation grant program because it duplicates a new mandatory grant program that will substantially increase funding for coal reclamation. Over the next 10 years, eligible States and Tribes will receive more than $2 billion in mandatory funding to prevent hazards from abandoned coal mines as well as mitigate existing hazards.

Background

The OSM coal reclamation grant program provides funding to States and Tribes to address hazards related to coal mines presenting an immediate danger to public health, safety, or general welfare. The program was established by the Surface Mining Control and Reclamation Act (SMCRA) in 1977.

The program is funded by assessing a reclamation fee on coal operators. The fees are deposited into the Abandoned Mine Land (AML) Fund and are then issued as grants to eligible States and Tribes. SMCRA requires that 50 percent of the fees collected from a given State or Tribe be allocated back to that State or Tribe for coal reclamation activities.

SMCRA was amended in 2006 to convert the grant program from discretionary to mandatory, and increase funding for coal reclamation from roughly $90 million a year to an average of $200 million a year for the next 10 years.

Department of the Interior: Discretionary Proposal
Rural Fire Assistance Program

Funding Summary
(In millions of dollars)

	2008 Enacted	2009 Proposed	Change From 2008
Budget Authority........................	6	---	-6

Administration Proposal and Impact

The Budget proposes to terminate the Rural Fire Assistance program, because the program is duplicative of other fire assistance grant programs. The items and activities funded by these grants, such as basic wildland fire safety equipment and tools, communication devices, wildland fire training, and community wildfire prevention and education activities, could be funded with existing Department of Homeland Security (DHS) and Department of Agriculture (USDA) Forest Service grant funding.

In lieu of these grants, the Department of the Interior (DOI) will focus more of its fire preparedness resources on training and certification of local firefighters so that they are qualified to assist on Federal fires. The Budget provides $866 million in funding for DOI's and USDA's preparedness activities and wildland firefighters.

Background

Begun as a pilot program in 2001, DOI's Rural Fire Assistance program provides grants to rural fire protection districts that serve communities of less than 10,000. The grants require a 10-percent local cost share and are used for the purchase of fire engines and other firefighting equipment, as well as for firefighter training and other related support. DHS' and USDA's Forest Service both operate grant programs that provide similar services to rural fire departments across the country. The Forest Service budget for this purpose is $73 million.   The proposed termination is consistent with the President's 2006, 2007, and 2008 Budgets. The program was not funded in 2007.

Department of Justice: Discretionary Proposal
State Criminal Alien Assistance Program

Funding Summary
(In millions of dollars)

	2008 Enacted	2009 Proposed	Change From 2008
Budget Authority..........................	410	---	-410

Administration Proposal and Impact

The Budget proposes to eliminate the State Criminal Alien Assistance Program (SCAAP), because the Administration believes that the Federal Government should focus on reducing illegal immigration rather than on reimbursing States/localities for the cost of incarcerating aliens who have committed State and local crimes.

While SCAAP partially reimburses States and counties for the cost of incarcerating illegal aliens who commit crimes, the program functions as an unfocused block grant, as funds can be used for any correctional purpose.

The Administration is committed to reducing illegal immigration by protecting the Nation's borders and enforcing immigration laws. The Budget reflects this commitment by proposing a 159-percent increase in Government-wide immigration enforcement and border security compared to 2001. These increases will support 2,200 new Border Patrol agents, as well as 1,000 new detention beds. Enhancing immigration enforcement addresses the root causes of incarcerated criminal aliens in State/local detention facilities. The Department of Justice's budget requests $100 million for the Southwest Border Enforcement Initiative, a comprehensive initiative within the Department to enforce Federal laws in the southwest border districts.

Background

The 1994 Crime Act authorizes the Department of Justice to assume responsibility for the cost of criminal, undocumented aliens incarcerated by States/localities for non-Federal offenses by providing reimbursement for their incarceration. Though the Act authorizes the Department to assume such a responsibility, the Department has never agreed to the interpretation by some States that the program should be viewed as an entitlement.

Only a few States benefit from more than two-thirds of the funds awarded. In 2007, California ($151 million), New York ($54 million), Texas ($29 million), and Florida ($25 million) received 69 percent of funding.

In 2005 the Department of Justice and OMB assessed the program using the Program Assessment Rating Tool and rated it Results Not Demonstrated because it lacks goals and performance metrics.

Department of Labor Discretionary Proposal
Denali Commission Job Training Earmark

Funding Summary
(In millions of dollars)

	2008 Enacted	2009 Proposed	Change From 2008
Budget Authority.........................	7	---	-7

Administration Proposal and Impact

The Budget proposes to terminate direct funding for the Department of Labor (DOL) Denali Commission Job Training congressional earmark; dedicated funding for job training is unnecessary and duplicative. Alaska will receive Federal support for job training and employment services through Workforce Investment Act (WIA) formula grants, Native Americans training grants, and a Job Corps center. The Budget requests $6 million -- $2 million in direct funding and $4 million in a trust fund – for the Denali Commission, which will allow it to continue the constructive role the Commission plays as a regional planner and coordinator of other Federal investments in Alaska.

Background

Established in 1998, the Denali Commission is a Federal partnership with Alaska to provide utilities, infrastructure, and economic support to distressed rural communities. Since 2004, the Congress has provided an earmark in DOL's appropriations for job training activities associated with Denali Commission projects. In 2004, this unrequested funding was $5 million, and in each of the years 2005 through 2008, it was $7 million. In addition to this earmark, the Denali Commission received appropriations totaling $26 million in 2008.

This earmark is duplicative of several related DOL programs. Alaska and its citizens receive millions of dollars from the Federal Government for job training and employment services through DOL's WIA programs. For instance, in program year 2007, Alaska received formula grants totaling $12.7 million to provide job training and employment services to adults and youth. Further, certain Alaskan Tribes receive funding from the WIA Native American program. During the last round of grant awards, Alaskan Tribes and other entities serving Native Americans received $2.8 million for job training and employment activities. Alaska also has a federally funded Job Corps center in Palmer.

Recent DOL research indicates that Alaska carries unexpended balances in their WIA accounts. If the State has not exhausted its regular WIA appropriations, there is little reason to continue providing even more funds through this earmark.

Department of Labor Discretionary Proposal
Migrant and Seasonal Farmworkers Training Program

Funding Summary
(In millions of dollars)

	2008 Enacted	2009 Proposed	Change From 2008
Budget Authority........................	80	---	-80

Administration Proposal and Impact

The Budget proposes to terminate the Department of Labor's (DOL's) Migrant and Seasonal Farmworker program, which provides grants to organizations to provide training, employment and other services to farmworkers. Program participants could be better served through the nationwide system of more than 3,500 One Stop Career Centers and other Federal programs.

DOL has taken a number of steps to better integrate farmworkers into the broader workforce system, such as: 1) holding forums to inform agricultural employers about the workforce system; 2) allowing workforce boards, which operate One Stop Career Centers, to be eligible grantees to provide services to farmworkers; and 3) overseeing a project designed to demonstrate the feasibility of local workforce boards providing year-round services to farmworkers.

Background

This program is intended to provide job training, employment assistance, and other services to help economically disadvantaged farmworkers and their families achieve economic self-sufficiency by strengthening their ability to gain stable employment. A Program Assessment Rating Tool assessment found that the program is ineffective in achieving these goals and that its services duplicate those provided by other Federal programs.

In addition, the program does not focus sufficiently on job training and employment, as one of its central goals is to help participants pursue job training and employment assistance that will help them to gain stable, year-round employment. Despite this, fewer than 40 percent of program participants receive job training, and only 26 percent enter unsubsidized employment. Each year, more than 50 percent of the approximately 30,000 participants receive only supportive services like emergency cash assistance – services already funded through other Federal programs.

The grants are competitively awarded, but because so few apply, there has not always been adequate competition.

Department of Labor: Discretionary Proposal
Susan Harwood Training Grants

Funding Summary
(In millions of dollars)

	2008 Enacted	2009 Proposed	Change From 2008
Budget Authority..........................	10	---	-10

Administration Proposal and Impact

The Budget proposes to terminate the Susan Harwood Training Grant program in the Occupational Safety and Health Administration (OSHA) and redirect these funds to compliance assistance activities such as web-based tools, which are a more cost-effective strategy for disseminating safety and health information. Terminating this program would not compromise OSHA's delivery of compliance assistance, outreach, and training to employers and workers.

Background

OSHA's Susan Harwood Training Grant program was established in 1978 to provide one- to five-year competitive grants to nonprofit organizations to develop or conduct training programs in selected safety and health topics.

Beginning in 2003 and in each year thereafter, the Administration has proposed terminating the Harwood Training Grant program for three main reasons: 1) it duplicates other, more cost-effective OSHA safety education activities; 2) there are no data to suggest that the program is successful or serves an unmet need; and 3) grantees have experienced difficulties recruiting employers and employees to attend the Harwood training programs.

Department of Labor: Discretionary Proposal
Work Incentive Grants

Funding Summary
(In millions of dollars)

	2008 Enacted	2009 Proposed	Change From 2008
Budget Authority..........................	14	---	-14

Administration Proposal and Impact

The Budget proposes to terminate funding for Work Incentive Grants, a pilot program that has accomplished its mission of demonstrating new approaches to improving the accessibility of One-Stop services for job seekers with disabilities. Separate grants are no longer needed to promote accessibility; States and localities can now implement these approaches as part of their regular support for the One-Stop Career centers.

Ending this program will not detrimentally affect one-stop accessibility for job-seekers with disabilities. The Department of Education's Vocational Rehabilitation State Grants program will continue to provide technical assistance to One-Stop Centers on program accessibility. More importantly, Section 504 of the Rehabilitation Act mandates that organizations that receive Federal funds be accessible to people with disabilities.

Background

The Work Incentive Grants program was created in 2000 as a pilot program to strengthen the capacity of the One-Stop Career Centers – centers that link job seekers and workers with job opportunities, training, and other services – to serve people with disabilities. The program provides competitive grants to State and local entities to demonstrate innovative approaches to improving one-stop services for job seekers with disabilities. Most recently, the program has worked with the Social Security Administration to fund "disability program navigators," or advocates who are responsible for bringing greater awareness of disability-related workforce issues to One-Stop staff. Work Incentive Grants have supported system and capacity building and improved the physical accessibility of One-Stops, but do not finance direct services to job seekers with disabilities.

Environmental Protection Agency: Discretionary Proposal
Targeted Watershed Grants

Funding Summary
(In millions of dollars)

	2008 Enacted	2009 Proposed	Change From 2008
Budget Authority..........................	10	---	-10

Administration Proposal and Impact

The 2009 Budget proposes to terminate the Environmental Protection Agency's (EPA's) Targeted Watersheds Grants program to improve the efficiency of EPA water quality programs. These grants are not necessary since EPA can provide watershed restoration funds more efficiently through its core water quality programs.

Background

The Targeted Watersheds Grants program provides competitive grants to State, local, and tribal governments and non-governmental organizations for community-based watershed restoration. The program was established in the 2003 Budget and has provided funding to organizations for projects that implement watershed restoration and build capacity in communities. Recently, appropriations report language carved out Target Watersheds funding to specific geographic regions, compromising the competitive nature of the program. EPA can more efficiently fund watershed restoration through its core water quality programs.

Environmental Protection Agency: Discretionary Proposal
Unrequested Water Infrastructure Projects

Funding Summary
(In millions of dollars)

	2008 Enacted	2009 Proposed	Change From 2008
Budget Authority..........................	133	---	-133

Administration Proposal and Impact

The Budget proposes to eliminate the funds that the Congress earmarked for specific water infrastructure projects in the Environmental Protection Agency's (EPA's) State and Tribal Assistance Grants (STAG) account. Earmarking circumvents the normal allocation and State priority setting processes and diverts funding from other higher priority projects.

Background

Earmarks in EPA's STAG account are targeted for wastewater or drinking water infrastructure projects. They are not subject to State priority setting, which typically ensures that cost-effective and higher priority activities are funded first. Such earmarks require even more oversight and technical assistance from EPA than standard grants because many recipients are unprepared to spend or manage the funds. Earmark projects also generally take several years to complete, requiring EPA resources for an extended period of time. The 2009 Budget provides $1.4 billion within STAG for non-earmarked water infrastructure grants.

Commission of Fine Arts: Discretionary Proposal
National Capital Arts and Cultural Affairs

Funding Summary
(In millions of dollars)

	2008 Enacted	2009 Proposed	Change From 2008
Budget Authority..........................	8	---	-8

Administration Proposal and Impact

The 2009 Budget proposes to terminate the Commission of Fine Arts' (CFA's) National Capital Arts and Cultural Affairs (NCACA) grant program. The NCACA provides non-competitive grants for general operating support to Washington, D.C. arts and other cultural organizations. In general, affected institutions may also apply for Federal funding from other national competitive grant programs. It at least one case, a grant recipient (The Kennedy Center) already receives an annual appropriation for operations and maintenance. In addition to the annual appropriation (19 percent of income), the Kennedy Center receives income from donations (37 percent of income) and ticket sales (44 percent of income). The $500,000 NCACA grant represents only about 0.3 percent of the Kennedy Center's total revenue. The grants are awarded based on a pre-determined formula, not on performance-based merit, and there is no post-award follow-up to ensure that the grants are utilized for the purposes intended. The Budget proposes to eliminate funding for this program and to redirect the dollars to other higher priority programs while continuing to fund the core functions of CFA.

Background

NCACA, established by the Congress in 1986, is a non-competitive Federal grant program that provides funding to local D.C. arts institutions such as the Woolly Mammoth Theater, the Kennedy Center, the National Building Museum, the National Symphony Orchestra, and Ford's Theater, among others. It was transferred to CFA in 1988 from the National Endowment for the Humanities because of its "local" (non-State) nature. Rather than allocating funds based on performance or need, NCACA funds are allocated to 21 specific organizations based on a formula. The formula provides the largest amount of funds to those recipients with the highest annual income.

National Veterans Business Development Corporation: Discretionary Proposal

Funding Summary
(In millions of dollars)

	2008 Enacted	2009 Proposed	Change From 2008
Budget Authority.........................	1	---	-1

Administration Action

The Budget proposes to terminate the National Veterans Business Development Corporation (NVBDC). NVBDC's authorization specified that the Corporation should become financially self-sufficient by 2004. The program has not become self-sufficient or demonstrated that it is effective or necessary given existing Federal business development and training programs available to veterans through the Small Business Administration, Department of Veterans Affairs, and Department of Labor.

Background

NVBDC was created by P.L. 106-50 with the mandate to assist veterans through educational and business opportunities. While NVBDC has a few success stories, it does not systematically measure performance or outcomes and, therefore, is not able to demonstrate overall efficiency and effectiveness.

The program is duplicative of current Federal services available for veterans (and, in many cases, other small businesses), such as the loan, technical assistance, and surety bond programs of the Small Business Administration, and the employment training and career development assistance available from both the Departments of Veterans Affairs and Labor. Services at each one of these agencies reach thousands of veterans per year.

P.L. 106-50 specified that NVBDC should become financially self-sufficient by 2004. Therefore, it was the intent of the authorizers that NVBDC function as a private entity. Consistent with its original design, duplicative nature, and lack of effectiveness, the 2009 Budget provides no new funding for NVBDC.

Postal Service: Discretionary Proposal
Foregone Revenue Appropriation

Funding Summary
(In millions of dollars)

	2008 Enacted	2009 Proposed	Change From 2008
Budget Authority............................	29	---	-29

Administration Proposal and Impact

The Budget proposes to terminate the $29 million annual appropriation to reimburse the Postal Service (USPS) for revenue forgone for reduced rate mail. In 2003, the Administration worked with the Congress to re-estimate the pension costs of USPS, and the Congress enacted significant pension reforms. USPS benefited from pension savings of approximately $3 billion per year from 2003 through 2005 as a result of that legislation. In addition, postal reform legislation enacted in 2006 shifted the responsibility for funding the costs of military service pension credits from USPS to the Department of the Treasury and provided USPS greater pricing flexibility. The benefits of these reforms more than compensate USPS for the loss of this small forgone revenue appropriation.

Background

This program reimburses USPS for its prior years' lost revenue from legislatively mandated reduced rates for nonprofit mailers. In 1994, the Congress authorized $1.2 billion to be appropriated to USPS in $29 million increments over a 42-year period. As of the end of 2007, USPS has been reimbursed $406 million. The 2005 through 2008 Budgets have proposed to discontinue this reimbursement.

Discretionary Reductions

Discretionary Program Reductions
(Budget authority and obligation limitations in millions of dollars)

	2008 Enacted	2009 Request	2009 Less 2008
Program Reductions			
Department of Agriculture:			
Capital Improvement and Maintenance	484	406	-78
Distance Learning and Telemedicine Grants	30	20	-10
Forest Service Research and Grants	549	378	-171
Housing Repair Loans	10	5	-5
In-House Research Construction	47	-54	-101
In-House Research Programs	1,121	1,037	-84
Land Acquisition	43	6	-37
Multifamily Housing Revitalization Vouchers	28	-20	-48
National Forest System	1,470	1,350	-120
Water and Wastewater Grants	469	220	-249
Mandatory Reductions Providing Discretionary Offsets:			
Agricultural Management Assistance	---	-10	-10
Conservation Security Program	---	-80	-80
Environmental Quality Incentives Program	---	-220	-220
Funds for Strengthening Markets, Income, and Supply	---	-293	-293
Total, Department of Agriculture	**4,251**	**2,745**	**-1,506**
Department of Commerce:			
Economic Development Administration Grants	243	100	-143
Pacific Coastal Salmon Recovery	67	35	-32
Total, Department of Commerce	**310**	**135**	**-175**
Department of Education:			
21st Century Learning Opportunities	1,081	800	-281
Safe and Drug-Free Schools State Grants	295	100	-195
Teaching American History	118	50	-68
Total, Department of Education	**1,494**	**950**	**-544**
Department of Health and Human Services:			
Health Resources and Services Administration - Health Professions Grants	350	110	-240
Health Resources and Services Administration - Rural Health	175	25	-150
Substance Abuse and Mental Health Services Admin. - Pgms. of Reg'l and Nat'l Significance	889	639	-250
Mandatory Reduction Providing Discretionary Offsets:			
Social Services Block Grant	---	-500	-500
Total, Department of Health and Human Services	**1,414**	**274**	**-1,140**
Department of Homeland Security:			
State and Local Support Programs	4,105	2,200	-1,905
Total, Department of Homeland Security	**4,105**	**2,200**	**-1,905**
Department of Housing and Urban Development:			
Community Development Block Grant (including cancellation)	3,866	2,794	-1,072
Public Housing Capital Fund	2,439	2,024	-415
Total, Department of Housing and Urban Development	**6,305**	**4,818**	**-1,487**
Department of the Interior:			
Bureau of Indian Affairs - Roads	26	13	-13
U.S. Geological Survey - Mineral Resources Program	51	26	-25
Total, Department of the Interior	**77**	**39**	**-38**
Department of Labor:			
Indian and Native American Training Program	53	45	-8
International Labor Affairs Bureau	81	15	-66
Job Training Grants Consolidation	3,850	2,826	-1,024
Office of Disability Employment Policy	27	12	-15
Pilots, Demonstrations and Research	49	16	-33
Senior Community Service Employment	522	350	-172
Total, Department of Labor	**4,582**	**3,264**	**-1,318**

Discretionary Program Reductions
(Budget authority and obligation limitations in millions of dollars)

	2008 Enacted	2009 Request	2009 Less 2008
Department of Transportation:			
Amtrak (Intercity Passenger Rail)	1,355	900	-455
Essential Air Service	60	---	-60
Federal Aid Highways (obligation limitation)	41,216	39,399	-1,817
Railroad Rehabilitation and Improvement Financing Loan Program	---	---	---
Total, Department of Transportation	**42,631**	**40,299**	**-2,332**
Environmental Protection Agency:			
Clean Water State Revolving Fund	689	555	-134
Mexico Border	20	10	-10
Nonpoint Source Grants	201	185	-16
Total, Environmental Protection Agency	**910**	**750**	**-160**
National Aeronautics and Space Administration:			
Aeronautics Research	627	545	-82
New Millennium Program	58	4	-54
Total, National Aeronautics and Space Administration	**685**	**549**	**-136**
Small Business Administration:			
Microloan Program	17	---	-17
Total, Small Business Administration	**17**	**---**	**-17**
Other Agencies:			
Corporation for Public Broadcasting	448	200	-248
Delta Regional Authority	12	6	-6
Denali Commission Direct Grant-Making	26	6	-20
National Archives and Records Administration - National Historical Publications and Records Commission	10	---	-10
Total, Other Agencies	**496**	**212**	**-284**
Total, Program Reductions	**67,277**	**56,235**	**-11,042**

Department of Agriculture: Discretionary Proposal
Forest Service Capital Improvement and Maintenance

Funding Summary
(In millions of dollars)

	2008 Enacted	2009 Proposed	Change From 2008
Budget Authority..........................	484	406	-78

Administration Proposal and Impact

The Budget proposes to reduce funding for Forest Service capital improvement and maintenance. The Budget reflects Forest Service continued use of authorities that permit the agency to apply proceeds from the sale of excess facilities to the replacement or rehabilitation of existing facilities. It also implements Program Assessment Rating Tool (PART) recommendations, includes incentives to optimize utilization and reduce costs, and sets priorities for addressing deferred maintenance.

Background

Funding provides for capital improvement and maintenance of Forest Service assets including facilities, roads, and trails. The program provides infrastructure that supports public, administrative, and recreation uses with minimal impact to ecosystem stability and conditions. Capital improvements may include new construction or the modification of facilities, roads, and trails. These changes may be necessary to change the function of facilities or to expand the facilities to accommodate increased capacity or meet emerging needs. Maintenance is divided into three primary areas: annual maintenance, deferred maintenance, and decommissioning.

A PART assessment recommended that the Forest Service develop long-term, outcome-based performance measures for roads, facilities, and trails. These measures should cover the full scope of the program and improve data quality in order to ensure that condition assessment surveys are accurate and drive management decisions regarding the construction, use, maintenance, and disposal of agency assets.

Department of Agriculture: Discretionary Proposal
Distance Learning and Telemedicine Grant Program

Funding Summary
(In millions of dollars)

	2008 Enacted	2009 Proposed	Change From 2008
Budget Authority........................	30	20	-10

Administration Proposal and Impact

The Budget proposes to provide $20 million for Distance Learning and Telemedicine (DLT) grants. Projected carryover balances and the 2009 request will maintain the available funding at approximately $25 million, the traditional funding level for this program.

Background

The purpose of the DLT Grant Program is to encourage and improve distance learning and telemedicine services in rural areas through the use of telecommunications, computer networks, and related advanced technologies by students, teachers, medical professionals, and rural residents. The Administration has routinely requested, and the Congress has provided, $25 million for this program. However, the Congress provided $30 million in 2008.

Department of Agriculture: Discretionary Proposal
Forest Service Research and Grants

Funding Summary
(In millions of dollars)

	2008 Enacted	2009 Proposed	Change From 2008
Budget Authority..........................	549	378	-171

Administration Proposal and Impact

The Budget proposes to reduce funding for Forest Service research and grants in order to focus resources on management of the federally-owned assets of the National Forest System. Funding is provided for priority research and technical assistance to non-industrial private forest landowners. In the 2009 Budget, the Budget provides a program level that enables the Department of Agriculture to provide financial assistance on high priority cooperative conservation projects.

Background

Research by the Forest Service provides information and solutions to sustain forests and rangelands that restore healthy forests and protect communities. Approximately 363 million acres, or 48 percent, of all forestland in the United States is under non-industrial or private family ownership. Forest Service grants and technical assistance are provided to states and non-industrial private forest landowners to help sustain the Nation's urban and rural forests, as well as to protect communities and the environment from wildland fires, insects, disease, and invasive plants. The Forest Service has made only marginal progress with improving program performance and allocating resources to address national priorities in the most effective and efficient manner.

Department of Agriculture: Discretionary Proposal
Housing Repair Direct Loan Program

Funding Summary
(In millions of dollars)

	2008 Enacted	2009 Proposed	Change From 2008
Budget Authority........................	10	5	-5
Loan Level.................................	34	18	-16

Administration Proposal and Impact

This decrease in housing repair loans reflects the preference of qualified recipients for grants over loans. While the loans are being decreased, a separate program that provides repair grants is essentially maintained at slightly above the 2008 enacted level of $30 million. The small redirection in loan subsidy allows the Department to prioritize funding within its rural housing programs to support current policies and objectives. The requested $18 million in loan level will ensure that sufficient assistance is provided to the lowest income homeowners with essential repairs.

Background

Rural Housing Repair Loans provide subsidized financing for repairs to improve or modernize a home, or to remove health and safety hazards. These loans are available to very low-income rural residents who own and occupy a dwelling in need of repairs. This is a one percent loan that may be repaid over a 20-year period. A rural area for this program is defined as a population of 20,000 or less.

Department of Agriculture: Discretionary Proposal
In-House Research Facility Construction

Funding Summary
(In millions of dollars)

	2008 Enacted	2009 Proposed	Change From 2008
Budget Authority..........................	47	-54	-101
Unrequested projects/prior balances................................	44	-67	-111
Funding for Athens Facilities.......	3	13	+10

Administration Proposal and Impact

The Budget proposes to cancel the $67 million in unobligated balances generated by congressional add-ons through 2006. This represents funding for 27 projects located in 18 States. None of these projects has more than 17 percent of the funding required to begin the project. Total funding to complete these projects is $511 million.

The Budget proposes to fund the remaining planning and design needs of a Biocontainment Laboratory and Consolidated Research Facility in Athens, Georgia ($13 million). By increasing and providing state-of-the-art biocontainment capacity and research space, this facility will help respond effectively to the threat of highly virulent poultry diseases, such as avian influenza, Exotic Newcastle Disease, and West Nile Virus, which is a high priority homeland security goal.

Background

This program funds construction for Department of Agriculture research facilities. The Administration has generally proposed funding for a phase of a single project, such as the National Centers for Animal Health (Ames, IA) or the Biocontainment Laboratory and Consolidated Poultry Research Facility (Athens, GA) that meets a national need such as animal diseases. However, the Congress regularly provides moderate funding for approximately 20 or more individual projects each year, resulting in large unobligated balances. While a project cannot begin until sufficient funds are accumulated to complete a phase, individual projects rarely receive the total amount of funding necessary to start construction. The 2008 Budget proposed to offset funding for the Athens laboratory ($16 million) by canceling an equal amount of funding for balances from unrequested projects. The 2009 Budget proposes to cancel all earmark balances ($67 million) through 2006. (Note: there were no earmarked funds appropriated in 2007).

Department of Agriculture: Discretionary Proposal
In-House Research Projects

Funding Summary
(In millions of dollars)

	2008 Enacted	2009 Proposed	Change From 2008
Budget Authority..........................	1,121	1,037	-84

Administration Proposal and Impact

The Budget proposes to reduce funding for lower priority research projects and earmarks, while increasing funding for new and expanded research in priority areas such as food safety, obesity prevention, crop and animal diseases, bioenergy, and bioproducts. This proposal will improve the relevance, performance and quality of Department of Agriculture (USDA) research and focus resources on the most pressing problems and issues.

Background

USDA has approximately 1,200 in-house research projects at about 110 locations, employing about 8,500 USDA scientists and support staff. Within available funding, the Administration has proposed to target resources to high priority research areas, while reducing congressional add-ons. The Administration's position is that Federal research dollars should be spent on the highest priority national needs, rather than on specific projects that are not national in scope.

Department of Agriculture: Discretionary Proposal
Forest Service Land Acquisition

Funding Summary
(In millions of dollars)

	2008 Enacted	2009 Proposed	Change From 2008
Budget Authority........................	43	6	-37

Administration Proposal and Impact

The Budget proposes to reduce funding for Forest Service land acquisition. The Budget focuses on taking proper care of the currently-owned National Forests System (NFS) lands rather than new acquisitions. By focusing on NFS lands already owned, the 2009 Budget enables the Department of Agriculture to conduct land exchanges that protect critical forest resources and reduces future management, maintenance, and protection costs.

The Budget also reflects implementation of Program Assessment Rating Tool recommendations that include establishing national priorities for the allocation of funds, linking the agency strategic plan with land acquisition goals, and improving efficiency.

Background

The Land Acquisition program provides for the acquisition of lands, waters, and related interests within the National Forest System for outdoor recreation; conservation of wildlife and threatened and endangered species habitat; watershed protection; resource management; healthy forests and grasslands; and public access.

Department of Agriculture: Discretionary Proposal
Multifamily Housing Revitalization Vouchers

Funding Summary
(In millions of dollars)

	2008 Enacted	2009 Proposed	Change From 2008
Budget Authority.........................	28	-20	-48

Administration Proposal and Impact

No new funding is requested for the rural multifamily housing revitalization voucher program because it is expected that 2009 needs will be met by carryover funds. In addition, a further reduction is taken through a proposed rescission of $20 million in unobligated balances in the account. The demand for the voucher program is less than expected because fewer landlords have chosen to prepay their USDA loans (resulting in fewer than expected displaced tenants), and it is expected that the carryover balances will not be needed in 2009.

Background

The multifamily housing revitalization voucher program is designed to protect tenants against possible displacement in situations where prepayment or foreclosure occurs in a Department of Agriculture (USDA) financed multifamily housing complex. The program provides short-term voucher-based rental assistance for up to 36 months while tenants decide on their long-term housing options. In addition to this voucher program, the Administration is providing $100 million for a new voucher program authorized under the Rental Assistance Program that will, for select properties, provide vouchers to tenants in lieu of rental assistance grants to property owners. These "rental assistance vouchers" are to be used in place of regular rental assistance grants on USDA-financed properties, as compared to the "revitalization vouchers," which go to tenants who are displaced by owners at the time of payoff.

Department of Agriculture: Discretionary Proposal
National Forest System

Funding Summary
(In millions of dollars)

	2008 Enacted	2009 Proposed	Change From 2008
Budget Authority.........................	1,470	1,350	-120

Administration Proposal and Impact

The Budget proposes to reduce funding for the National Forest System. The reduction reflects organizational improvements permitting the Forest Service to become a more effective, efficient, and integrated operation. The request increases the percentage of budgetary resources going to on-the-ground foresters and will improve overall performance by reducing overhead, streamlining decision-making, and implementing a new forest planning process.

Background

The Forest Service's National Forest System (NFS) covers 193 million acres of land, an area equivalent to the size of Texas. The National Forest System account funds 155 National Forests and 20 National Grasslands managed under multiple-use and sustained-yield principles. Large overhead and indirect costs associated with national headquarters and regional offices have impeded performance and reduced funding available for managing the resources of the National Forests. The Forest Service has set a goal of reducing its indirect costs, and the Budget builds on this effort by increasing Forest Service administrative efficiencies and allowing the Forest Service to direct its work in a manner that is more integrated with its on-the-ground mission responsibilities.

Department of Agriculture: Discretionary Proposal
Rural Water and Wastewater Grants

Funding Summary
(In millions of dollars)

	2008 Enacted	2009 Proposed	Change From 2008
Budget Authority..........................	469	220	-249

Administration Proposal and Impact

The decrease in the Water and Wastewater Grants is a direct outgrowth of the low interest rates currently available. The Department of Agriculture (USDA) combines grant funding with loans to ensure that communities can successfully repay their loans at reasonable user rates. The relatively low interest rates currently available on loans allow more projects to be feasible with less grant funding. Consequently, the overall program will be able to operate at a higher loan to grant ratio, allowing USDA to serve more communities with less budget authority overall.

In conjunction with this decrease in grant funding, the Budget proposes an increase in the Water and Wastewater Direct Loan program (not shown above). The total program level (grants and loan level combined) is $1.6 billion, a $33 million increase over 2008. In addition, State directors have authority to transfer a portion of the funding between the loans and grants, allowing them to target resources to state and local priorities.

Background

The Water and Wastewater Grants are authorized in the Consolidated Farm and Rural Development Act, as amended. These funds are available to low-income rural communities of 10,000 or less people. They are typically used in conjunction with a Water and Wastewater Direct Loan. The grants are used to buy down the loan payment to a reasonable rate, as determined by USDA. The grant is usually for 35-45 percent of the project cost (it can be up to 75 percent). Loans are for 40 years with interest rates based on a three-tiered structure (poverty, intermediate, and market) depending on community income. The program finances drinking water, sewer, solid waste disposal, and storm drainage facilities. In order to qualify, applicant communities must be unable to finance their needs through their own resources or with credit from commercial lenders. Priority is given to loans serving smaller communities that have greater financial need, based on their median household income, poverty levels, and size of service population.

Department of Agriculture:
Mandatory Reductions Providing Discretionary Offsets

Funding Summary
(In millions of dollars)

	2008 Enacted	2009 Proposed	Change From 2008
Funds for Strengthening Markets, Income and Supply....................	---	-293	-293
Environmental Quality Incentives Program.............................	---	-220	-220
Conservation Security Program...	---	-80	-80
Agricultural Management Assistance...........................	===	-10	-10
Total, BA Offsets.................	---	**-603**	**-603**

Administration Proposal and Impact

The 2009 Budget proposes to cancel unneeded funding and funding for lower-priority and duplicative programs authorized by existing farm legislation. An additional $39 million is proposed in discretionary terminations as discussed on page 10. The proposed cancellation of mandatory funding would affect the programs listed below. In the past, the Congress has adopted similar savings proposed by the Administration:

- *Funds for Strengthening Markets, Income and Supply* – This program aims to increase the domestic consumption of agricultural commodities through the purchase and donation of surplus fruits and vegetables. Program funds have also been used to provide disaster assistance to producers suffering from natural disasters. The budget proposes to cancel $293 million made available in 2009.

- *Environmental Quality Incentives Program* – This program provides financial and technical assistance to farmers and ranchers to install conservation measures on working lands to address a variety of natural resource concerns, including air, soil, and water quality. The budget proposes to cancel $220 million out of $1.27 billion available in 2009.

- *Conservation Security Program* – This program provides financial rewards to good conservation stewards and also provides additional incentives for the program participants to achieve higher levels of environmental performance. The budget proposes to cancel $80 million out of $440 million made available in 2009.

- *Agricultural Management Assistance* – The program provides assistance to agricultural producers to mitigate financial risk by using conservation measures to reduce soil erosion and improve water quality. The budget proposes to cancel $10 million made available in 2009.

Background

Similar to previous Administration proposals, the Budget includes proposals to permanently cancel mandatory funds that provide for a discretionary offset. Many of these programs are more appropriately funded with discretionary resources, and cancelling these funds offsets higher-priority discretionary spending. The Agricultural Management Assistance program is duplicative of other conservation programs. For the Environmental Quality Incentives Program and the Conservation Security Program, the 2009 budget assumes a slower increase in funding than the annual authorized level. Finally, the reduction to the Funds for Strengthening Markets, Income and Supply account reduces excess unobligated balances.

Department of Commerce: Discretionary Proposal
Economic Development Administration Grants

Funding Summary
(In millions of dollars)

	2008 Enacted	2009 Proposed	Change From 2008
Budget Authority..........................	243	100	-143

Administration Proposal and Impact

The Budget proposes to reduce the Economic Development Administration's (EDA's) grant funding to $100 million, $143 million below the 2008 enacted level. EDA's grant-making is duplicative of other Federal grant programs, most notably the Department of Agriculture's Rural Development and the Department of Housing and Urban Development's Community Development Block Grant (CDBG) programs. The proposed funding level will allow EDA to focus and prioritize funding to the Nation's most severely distressed communities and serve as a backstop to severe and sudden economic distress.

Background

Created in 1965, EDA's mission is to competitively award grants to regions experiencing economic distress or sudden economic downturns (i.e., due to plant or base closings). EDA invests in economic development projects focused on creating jobs and spurring private-sector investment.

A crosscutting Program Assessment Rating Tool review of community and economic development programs found that many had unclear objectives, did not coordinate effectively, and were unable to demonstrate measurable and sustained economic gains for communities. The Budget also proposes major reforms to CDBG, to better target resources to the most distressed communities, and to reduce or eliminate other duplicative development programs.

Department of Commerce: Discretionary Proposal
Pacific Coastal Salmon Recovery Fund

Funding Summary
(In millions of dollars)

	2008 Enacted	2009 Proposed	Change From 2008
Budget Authority.........................	67	35	-32

Administration Proposal and Impact

The Budget proposes to reduce funding for the Pacific Coastal Salmon Recovery Fund (PCSRF). The program provides matching funds for habitat restoration projects to State and tribal governments that in many cases are not Federal priorities. While the fund was intended to aid the recovery of salmon stocks listed as threatened and endangered, a significant portion is spent on enhancing streams in Alaska with robust salmon populations. The Budget proposes to reduce funding for this program and to redirect the dollars to higher priority programs.

Background

The PCSRF was established by the Congress in response to listings of about two dozen Pacific salmon stocks under the Endangered Species Act in the 1990s, and the 1999 Pacific Salmon Treaty Agreement between the United States and Canada. The PCSRF is used to conduct watershed assessments; develop recovery and restoration plans at a variety of scales; enhance salmon populations; educate constituencies; and conduct research to monitor, evaluate, and support salmon restoration and conservation efforts.

A program review in 2006 identified serious shortcomings in the projects funded by PCSRF. Alaska was a substantial recipient of funds, yet the State does not have listed salmon stocks and therefore does not conduct activities pursuant to the Endangered Species Act. Some of the projects in other states do not address the highest priority aspects of habitat restoration, and therefore have limited potential for recovering salmon stocks. Some programs lack performance measures.

From 2000 to 2008 the President has requested $771 million for the PCSRF program and the Congress has appropriated $726 million. The House of Representatives proposed $20 million for the PCSRF in 2007, noting that over $1.2 billion had been appropriated for the Department's Pacific Salmon programs since 2000.

Department of Education: Discretionary Proposal
21st Century Learning Opportunities (formerly 21st Century Community Learning Centers)

Funding Summary
(In millions of dollars)

	2008 Enacted	2009 Proposed	Change From 2008
Budget Authority.........................	1,081	800	-281

Administration Proposal and Impact

The Budget provides $800 million to transform the 21st Century Community Learning Centers (CCLC) program to better support and expand ongoing state efforts to improve the academic achievement of disadvantaged students. The reformed and renamed 21st Century Learning Opportunities program would give parents the opportunity to select from a greater array of high-quality after-school and summer-school providers, including faith-based and community organizations. Operated as a scholarship program for disadvantaged K-12 students, the program would provide direct aid to families seeking extended-learning opportunities for their children. A key reform of the program is ensuring that these out-of-school opportunities are designed to primarily improve educational achievement consistent with State standards. The reauthorized program would continue to allocate funding by formula to States, which would award competitive grants to public or private nonprofit organizations to administer scholarships for students from low-income families who attend schools that have been identified for school improvement, corrective action, or restructuring under No Child Left Behind (NCLB), or who attend schools with a graduation rate of less than 60 percent.

Background

The evaluation of the 21st CCLC program as it operated prior to the No Child Left Behind Act revealed weaknesses in program implementation and outcomes. Program participants did not attain higher levels of achievement as measured by reading test scores or grades in mathematics, science, social studies, and English compared to students in the control group. Although NCLB attempted to focus the program on academic improvement, program performance data indicate little or no improvement. These data show either that the program has not improved academic outcomes since 2004, or, where there has been some improvement, performance targets have not been met. This supports a strategy of reforming the program to focus much more on student achievement, and to place a greater emphasis on accountability through parental choice.

Department of Education: Discretionary Proposal
Safe and Drug-Free Schools State Grants

Funding Summary
(In millions of dollars)

	2008 Enacted	2009 Proposed	Change From 2008
Budget Authority.........................	295	100	-195

Administration Proposal and Impact

The Budget requests $100 million for the Safe and Drug-Free Schools (SDFS) State Grants program, $195 million below the 2008 level. The Administration, as part of No Child Left Behind reauthorization, is proposing legislative reforms to significantly change the structure of this program to focus resources on building State capacity to assist school districts in creating safe, drug-free schools and secure school environments. Under the Administration's reauthorization proposal, the Department of Education would allocate SDFS State Grant funds by formula to State Educational Agencies, which would use the funds to provide school districts support for the implementation of effective models that reflect scientifically-based research.

Background

The SDFS State Grants program as currently structured provides formula grants to States and school districts for an array of activities intended to reduce youth crime and drug abuse. Even though the State grant program is more than 20 years old, it cannot demonstrate it has had a positive impact on reducing drug use and violence. A 2001 RAND study determined that the structure of the program is fundamentally flawed. It concluded that SDFS State Grants, which distribute funds according to a formula, are spread too thinly to support quality interventions. SDFS State Grants provide about 64 percent of local educational agencies with allocations of less than $10,000 (amounts typically too small to mount comprehensive and effective drug and school safety programs). The Department of Education and the Office of Management and Budget first assessed the program using the Program Assessment Rating Tool (PART) in 2004 and reassessed the program in 2006. The most recent PART assessment found the program was unable to demonstrate results. This program received its first significant reduction in 2004 (-$28 million) and since then it has been reduced by $146 million, or 33 percent.

Department of Education: Discretionary Proposal
Teaching American History

Funding Summary
(In millions of dollars)

	2008 Enacted	2009 Proposed	Change From 2008
Budget Authority..........................	118	50	-68

Administration Proposal and Impact

The Budget requests $50 million for the Teaching American History program, $68 million below the 2008 level. The number of quality applications for assistance under this program has been insufficient to justify continuing the 2008 level of funding. The request should be sufficient to fund all high-scoring applicants, ensuring that the program effectively supports projects that have well-conceived strategies for increasing teacher knowledge and student achievement and a strong management plan for achieving that goal.

Background

The Teaching American History program supports competitive three-year grants to local educational agencies to promote the teaching of American history in elementary and secondary schools as a separate academic subject. Starting in 2008, the Department may extend these grants for two additional years if the grantee is performing. Grants are used to improve the quality of history instruction by supporting training for teachers of American history (including elementary school teachers who teach the general curriculum).

The number of quality applications for assistance has been insufficient to justify continuing the current level of funding. For example, as in 2005 and 2006, the Department estimates that only about 50 percent of successful applications in fiscal year 2007 were of high quality. As a result, the Department has had to fund many lower-quality grant applications.

Department of Health and Human Services: Discretionary Proposal
Health Professions Grants

Funding Summary
(In millions of dollars)

	2008 Enacted	2009 Proposed	Change From 2008
Budget Authority......................	350	110	-240

Administration Proposal and Impact

The Budget requests $110 million for health professions training, phasing out most health profession grants, and directing resources to activities that are more effective in placing health care providers in medically-underserved communities. Continuing subsidies to persuade individuals to enter well-paid medical careers is not the best use of Federal funds, particularly when there is no documented national shortage of physicians. While there are regions and pockets of the Nation that face shortages, only two of every ten providers who benefit from these training grants enter shortage areas. The Budget invests $110 million for the education and training of registered nurses, including scholarships and loan repayments in exchange for a service commitment in an underserved community.

Background

The Health Professions training grants assist academic institutions to help meet the costs of training and educating students to become nurses, doctors, dentists, and other health professionals. These grants were authorized in the early 1960s, partially in response to an anticipated national shortage of physicians that does not exist today. Between 1992 and 2004, the U.S. physician population increased by 36 percent, over twice the rate of growth of the total population. Evaluations have not linked the Health Professions training grants to changes in supply, distribution, and minority representation of physicians and other health professionals. These finding are documented in the Program Assessment Rating Tool (PART) assessment that the Department of Health and Human Services and the Office of Management and Budget completed, which resulted in Health Professions training grants receiving an Ineffective PART rating.

Department of Health and Human Services: Discretionary Proposal
Rural Health

Funding Summary
(In millions of dollars)

	2008 Enacted	2009 Proposed	Change From 2008
Budget Authority......................	175	25	-150

Administration Proposal and Impact

The Budget requests $25 million for the Health Resources and Services Administration's (HRSA) Rural Health activities. Consistent with previous Budgets, funding is eliminated for activities that no longer support a continuing need or that duplicate other Department of Health and Human Services (HHS) and Federal agencies' programs, including: (1) rural health outreach grants; (2) rural access to emergency devices; (3) hospital flexibility grants; and (4) the Denali Commission. The Budget continues to support State rural health offices and rural health policy research. Funding is also included for radiological and black lung diseases that disproportionately affect rural areas. The Budget proposes over $2 billion for Health Centers. More than 50 percent of Health Center sites are located in rural areas and seven million low-income and underserved individuals will receive health care from these sites in 2008. In addition, Medicare, through the Critical Access Hospital (CAH) program, finances payments that improve the profitability of many rural hospitals and ensure beneficiary access to care.

Background

HRSA's Rural Health activities fund a variety of grants designed to improve health care in rural areas. Many of these grant activities no longer support an existing and/or specific purpose. For instance, the Budget proposes to eliminate funding for Rural Health Hospital Flexibility Grants that are designed to help States determine if rural hospitals might benefit from conversion to CAH Status. The majority of these conversions have already taken place. Also proposed for elimination is funding to help communities purchase defibrillators, as much of the demand for these medical devices has been met through prior grants. This activity has received $272 million in funding since 2000. In addition, the Budget eliminates funding for rural health outreach grants, as many other activities support rural health. A study found that HHS administers 225 health and social services programs that provide resources to rural areas. The Medicare Modernization Act (MMA) contained several provisions to support rural health, for example, increasing Medicare CAH payments to 101 percent of costs and broadening eligibility criteria for CAHs. The number of CAHs receiving enhanced Medicare payments has grown significantly since the passage of MMA.

Department of Health and Human Services: Discretionary Proposal
Substance Abuse and Mental Health Services Administration -- Programs of Regional and National Significance

Funding Summary
(In millions of dollars)

	2008 Enacted	2009 Proposed	Change From 2008
Budget Authority..........................	889	639	-250
Substance Abuse Prevention and Treatment PRNS	*590*	*484*	*-106*
Mental Health PRNS.............	*299*	*155*	*-144*

Administration Proposal and Impact

The 2009 Budget reduces or eliminates funding for less effective or redundant activities within the Substance Abuse and Mental Health Services Administration's Substance Abuse and Mental Health Programs of Regional and National Significance (PRNS). The 2009 Budget directs resources to activities that have demonstrated improvements in mental health and substance abuse outcomes and increased treatment capacity. For example, the 2009 Budget eliminates grant activities that have not met performance goals such as the State Incentive grants for Transformation, Pregnant and Postpartum Women, and the Recovery Community Services Program. These reductions are offset by increased funds for new Targeted Capacity Expansion (TCE) grants, Drug Court services, and the Substance Abuse Prevention and Treatment Block Grant. TCE grants will address emerging mental health and substance abuse needs, which could include school violence, post-traumatic stress disorder, alcohol abuse or other issues as determined by States and local communities.

Background

The Substance Abuse and Mental Health PRNS fund a diverse array of activities ranging from direct services to disseminating information on effective strategies. The 2009 Budget focuses resources on areas that directly expand access to drug treatment and prevention activities such as drug court treatment services and screening, brief intervention, referral, and treatment activities. The Budget redirects some of the Mental Health PRNS funds to more effective programs that serve similar populations such as the Community Mental Health Services Program (CMHSP) and the Projects for Assistance in Transition from Homelessness. Both of these activities have improved health outcomes, enhanced accountability, exceeded performance targets, and leveraged Federal resources through a matching element.

Previous Budgets have proposed reductions to this portfolio and the Budget reproposes $77 million in reductions from the 2008 Budget. A 2005 Program Assessment Rating Tool assessment completed by the Department of Health and Human Services and OMB found that not all Mental Health PRNS activities were effective or efficient at improving mental health services.

Department of Health and Human Services: Discretionary Proposal
Social Services Block Grant

Funding Summary
(In millions of dollars)

	2008 Enacted	2009 Proposed	Change From 2008
Budget Authority........................	---	-500	-500

Administration Proposal and Impact

The Budget proposes to reduce funding for the Social Services Block Grant by $500 million, to $1.2 billion, through appropriations for 2009, and to terminate authorization of SSBG for 2010 and beyond. Federal support for social services will continue through other funding streams. The program lacks performance measures or other means to demonstrate that activities supported by SSBG funds are producing results. SSBG overlaps with other Federal social service programs that serve low-income and needy families including Federal child care and child welfare programs, Temporary Assistance for Needy Families, and programs that provide services to the elderly.

Background

The Social Services Block Grant was established in 1981 to help States provide a broad range of social services to help needy families achieve economic self-sufficiency, to prevent or remedy neglect or abuse, and secure institutional care, when appropriate. States receive a capped block grant with few Federal requirements. While this approach maximizes State flexibility to determine what services to provide and whom to serve, it does not ensure that funds are directed most effectively.

Department of Homeland Security: Discretionary Proposal
State and Local Support Programs

Funding Summary
(In millions of dollars)

	2008 Enacted	2009 Proposed	Change From 2008
Budget Authority........................	4,105	2,200	-1,905

Administration Proposal and Impact

The Budget proposes to reduce and consolidate Homeland Security State and local support funding by eliminating duplicative initiatives and reducing programs that are not allocated solely on the basis of risk. The overall funding level for these programs has been reduced from 2008 enacted levels, but remains consistent with the amount requested in 2008.

Background

State and local support programs provide grants, training, exercises, and other assistance to State and local partners to build national capabilities to prevent, protect against, respond to, and recover from terrorist attacks and other major events. From 2001 through 2008, DHS will have administered over $27 billion, primarily in the form of grants, to support State and local preparedness. Although originally focused on immediate capital investment needs in the wake of the September 11th attacks, grantees in recent years have sought greater flexibility to support day-to-day operations as well as longer term communications and planning projects. Although some efforts are underway to measure the extent to which grant-funded projects improve national capabilities, there is no conclusive data available at present to measure achievements made through years of annual grant awards. Until a measurement process can be implemented nationwide, the relative value of funding the various preparedness projects supported through grants remains unclear.

Department of Housing and Urban Development: Discretionary Proposal Community Development Block Grant (CDBG)

Funding Summary
(In millions of dollars)

	2008 Enacted	2009 Proposed	Change From 2008
CDBG...............................	*3,866*	*3,000*	*-866*
Cancelled unobligated balances....	*---*	*-206*	*-206*
Budget Authority...........................	3,866	2,794	-1,072

Administration Proposal and Impact

The Budget proposes to fund the Community Development Block Grant (CDBG) program at $3.0 billion, equal to the 2008 request, and to cancel $206 million of prior year unobligated Economic Development Initiative and Neighborhood Initiative funds. The current CDBG program is not well-targeted; it is more than 30-year old formula awards more funds to wealthier communities than to many low-income communities. In addition, the results of its assistance have not been adequately demonstrated or reported. The Administration continues to support CDBG legislative reforms proposed in the CDBG Reform Act, which was transmitted to the Congress in June 2007. The reform legislation updates an outdated allocation formula that is over 30 years old, and adds other components that would improve the CDBG program. An improved CDBG formula would better target assistance to communities and regions experiencing greater economic distress and reduce or eliminate funding to more affluent communities. The proposed Challenge Grant fund would reward communities that strategically invest in projects that create conditions for community and economic progress. In addition, the Department of Housing and Urban Development (HUD) would establish ambitious performance measures and accountability standards for grantees that receive funds under the CDBG formula.

Background

The CDBG program was established in 1974 to provide flexible annual assistance to States and local governments to fund a wide range of community and economic development activities that principally benefit low- to moderate-income persons, eliminate slums and blight, and address urgent needs. The Administration's CDBG reform proposal was motivated by a crosscutting review of Federal community and economic development programs in 2004. This review found that many of these programs had unclear objectives, did not coordinate effectively, were duplicative, and were unable to demonstrate measurable and sustained economic gains for communities. As a part of this crosscut, HUD and Office of Management and Budget analysis also found that CDBG is ineffective. Specifically, the program's major problems include the lack of a clear purpose and annual and long-term outcome measures; weak targeting of funds to areas of greatest need; and the inability to produce transparent information on results.

Department of Housing and Urban Development: Discretionary Proposal
Public Housing Capital Fund

Funding Summary
(In millions of dollars)

	2008 Enacted	2009 Proposed	Change From 2008
Budget Authority..........................	2,439	2,024	-415

Administration Proposal and Impact

The Budget proposes to reduce funding for public housing modernization and renovation by 17 percent from the 2008 level, because additional funds are not needed to cover the annual accrual of new capital needs. In 2009, the public housing authorities will also be able to fund additional capital needs by leveraging non-Federal investment dollars with their Capital Fund allocations.

Background

Since the 1930s, the Federal Government has supported the provision of housing assistance to low income households through the construction and operation of public housing. Although the housing is owned by local public housing authorities, Federal funds pay most operating costs as well as capital improvements. This arrangement often requires assisted households to live in less desirable locations and units in order to receive the housing subsidy. In contrast, other alternatives, such as the Department of Housing and Urban Development's (HUD's) Section 8 Tenant-based Assistance that the Budget proposes to increase and improve, allow families to select housing in neighborhoods with lower poverty and crime rates, as well as better schools. The Public Housing Capital Fund currently pays the annual and long-term modernization needs of 1.2 million public housing units. Public housing capital needs are estimated to accrue at a rate of about $2 billion a year.

The condition of public housing units in general has improved through modernization and, in other cases, demolition of units in the worst condition. Today, almost 86 percent of public housing units meet HUD's physical standards, compared to 82 percent in 2001. Since 1998, in order to pay for more comprehensive capital improvements, public housing authorities have been exercising flexible authority to use their Capital Fund dollars to leverage additional private bond or mortgage financing, repaid from capital funds. The use of such borrowing to capital needs has grown to over $2.9 billion.

Department of the Interior: Discretionary Proposal
Bureau of Indian Affairs' Roads Maintenance Program

Funding Summary
(In millions of dollars)

	2008 Enacted	2009 Proposed	Change From 2008
Budget Authority......................	26	13	-13

Administration Proposal and Impact

The Budget proposes to reduce funding for the Bureau of Indian Affairs (BIA) Roads Maintenance Program, which duplicates Department of Transportation (DOT) funding for Indian Reservation Roads (IRR). IRR funding has increased by 64 percent in five years, from $275 million in 2004 to $450 million in 2009. Since 2005, Tribes can use up to 25 percent of the IRR funds for road and bridge maintenance. The $13 million reduction in BIA roads maintenance funding is more than offset by over $110 million in DOT funding now available annually for maintenance.

Background

The BIA Roads Maintenance Program provides upkeep of approximately 27,000 BIA-owned roads and nearly 900 BIA-owned bridges constructed under the IRR program in Indian Country. The program is duplicative of DOT's much larger IRR program. This is the first year the BIA program has been recommended for a reduction. The proposal is consistent with the Administration's policy to gain efficiencies through consolidation of Federal programs while continuing to provide critically needed services to its constituents. The BIA program will undergo a Program Assessment Rating Tool review in 2008 to determine the future direction of the program.

Department of the Interior: Discretionary Proposal
United States Geological Survey – Mineral Resources Program

Funding Summary
(In millions of dollars)

	2008 Enacted	2009 Proposed	Change From 2008
Budget Authority..........................	51	26	-25

Administration Proposal and Impact

The Budget reduces the Mineral Resources Program (MRP) work on national and international mineral assessment products that benefit States, local governments, industry, and academia. State and local governments, industry, and universities could fund their own mineral assessments if they consider these products a priority. Remaining funds will focus on mineral surveys, studies, and commodity reports that are essential for ongoing Federal land management, regulatory, and remediation activities.

Background

The United States Geological Survey (USGS) maintains national databases and provides information on the location and quantity of minerals, formation of minerals, and the impact of mining on the environment. USGS has been responsible for these activities since they were transferred from the Bureau of Mines in 1996. MRP annually produces four to five systematic analyses, 700 to 720 mineral commodity reports and maintains five national geologic, geochemical, geophysical databases. MRP was originally proposed as a reduction in the 2006 Budget. Many of the program's products are used by states, local governments, industry, and academia rather than the Federal Government. The proposed funding level decreases the number of systematic analyses by MRP and reduces the number of formal workshops and training offered.

Department of Labor: Discretionary Proposal
Indian and Native Americans Program

Funding Summary
(In millions of dollars)

	2008 Enacted	2009 Proposed	Change From 2008
Budget Authority........................	53	45	-8

Administration Proposal and Impact

The Budget proposes to reduce funding for the Department of Labor's Indian and Native Americans Program, which funds competitive grants to federally-recognized tribes and other eligible entities to provide academic, literacy, and occupational training. Recent program management initiatives include the implementation of common performance measures, improvements to program reporting, enhanced review of grantees' financial management to ensure the efficient use of funds, and the use of technology to deliver services. These reforms should increase program efficiency and allow for increased performance at the 2009 funding level.

Background

Section 166 of the Workforce Investment Act (WIA) makes funds available to Indian tribes, tribal organizations, Alaska native entities, Indian controlled organizations serving Indians, or Native Hawaiian organizations to support employment and training activities for Indian, Alaska Native, or Native Hawaiian individuals.

A Program Assessment Rating Tool evaluation found the program to be Adequate, but noted several areas for improvement. In addition to implementing common performance measures, strengthening grantee reporting requirements, and using technology to deliver services, the Department of Labor should ensure that this program is aligned and works collaboratively with the numerous other Federal and State agencies and programs that provide employment, training, and other related services to Indian and Native American populations.

Department of Labor: Discretionary Proposal
International Labor Affairs Bureau

Funding Summary
(In millions of dollars)

	2008 Enacted	2009 Proposed	Change From 2008
Budget Authority….......................	81	15	-66

Administration Proposal and Impact

The Budget proposes $15 million for the International Labor Affairs Bureau (ILAB), returning the agency closer to its core mission of research and policy analysis. The Budget also eliminates the $40 million earmark enacted in 2008 for the International Labor Organization (ILO), which receives funding from other Federal agencies. In 2009, ILAB will continue to focus on administering over $280 million in projects that were launched in previous years, including projects to combat exploitive child labor and human trafficking, promote HIV/AIDS workplace education, and increase compliance with international labor standards. ILAB's budget also includes $1.5 million for child and forced labor-related activities authorized under the Trafficking Victims Protection Reauthorization Act.

Background

The Budget seeks to restore ILAB to its original mission of research, advocacy, and technical assistance by eliminating its grant making activities. Between 1996 and 2001, ILAB's funding rose by 1,500 percent, when the agency embarked on an expansive grant-making mission intended to combat international child labor, develop and disseminate AIDS prevention information in the international workplace, support core labor standards development, and provide bilateral technical assistance.

Foreign assistance is more appropriately financed and managed through the State Department, USAID, and other international agencies. This Administration has dramatically increased resources for foreign assistance, and official development assistance spending has grown at a faster rate than at any time since the Marshall Plan. Examples of such assistance include:

- Support to multilateral organizations such as the ILO, which seeks, as one of its priority activities, to end child labor. The Budget includes $77 million for our assessed dues to the general operations of the ILO within the Department of State's Contributions to International Organizations account.

- Programs to combat all forms of trafficking in persons (TIP). The Budget includes $15 million to support the activities of Global Trafficking in Persons Office at the Department of State. This level does not include additional resources to combat trafficking within country allocations requested elsewhere in the Budget for the Department of State.

- Assistance to expand access to quality basic education for children around the world. The Budget includes more than a four-fold increase in funding for basic education funding compared to 2001 levels. These levels include annual funding for the Africa Education Initiative, a multi-year $600 million Presidential initiative to increase access to quality basic education in 40 African countries.

- Broader efforts to promote human rights through the Department of State's Human Rights and Democracy Fund (HRDF). The Budget includes $60 million in the HRDF for these efforts to expand human rights and freedom.

Department of Labor: Discretionary Proposal
Job Training Grants Consolidation

Funding Summary
(In millions of dollars)

	2008 Enacted	2009 Proposed	Change From 2008
Budget Authority.........................	3,850	2,826	-1,024

Administration Proposal and Impact

The Budget proposes reforms to the Workforce Investment Act (WIA) that will provide training opportunities to more workers, provide States more flexibility to deliver services, and increase individual choice. The President's reforms would reduce duplication by consolidating multiple similar funding streams into a single State grant, limiting the amount of funds that could be spent on overhead, cutting Federal red tape, and creating Career Advancement Accounts – worker-directed accounts to give individuals the resources necessary to increase their skills and better compete for jobs. States would have more flexibility than they currently do to use funding to meet their unique workforce needs. This proposal is the same as the 2008 Budget proposal, with two exceptions. First, the 2009 legislative proposal includes a 20 percent State matching requirement, which will better integrate State and Federal workforce training resources. Second, the Budget proposes to eliminate the Employment Service State Grants, which duplicate services provided under the existing WIA programs.

Through these reforms, the President's proposal will save more than $1 billion in taxpayer dollars while significantly increasing the number of workers who have access to training opportunities.

Background

WIA authorizes formula grants to States and localities to provide job training and employment-related services to adults, dislocated workers, and disadvantaged youth. Services are provided primarily through a nationwide network of One-Stop Career Centers.

Currently, too few workers are trained and duplicative programs produce excessive overhead costs and administrative complexity. As a result, not enough of the close to $4 billion invested in the following Department of Labor programs goes to train workers: Dislocated Worker Assistance; Adult Employment and Training Activities; Youth Activities; Wagner-Peyser Employment Service State grants; Labor-Market Information funding; and State grants to administer the Work Opportunity tax credit. A recent Government Accountability Office study found that less than 40 percent of funding provided to local workforce investment boards was used to provide job training. Under the current system, 200,000 individuals receive training under these programs; the reforms would increase this number to 629,000, which includes 105,000 participants financed through State matching funds.

The Employment Service State Grants are also being eliminated, because they duplicate services provided under the Workforce Investment Act adult and dislocated worker programs. In addition, private entities provide some of the services that the ES has been delivering, with a fee charged to the job seeker and/or employer.

WIA's authorization expired in 2003. This reform builds on previous Administration proposals to reform and reauthorize WIA.

Department of Labor: Discretionary Proposal
Office of Disability Employment Policy

Funding Summary
(In millions of dollars)

	2008 Enacted	2009 Proposed	Change From 2008
Budget Authority........................	27	12	-15

Administration Proposal and Impact

The Budget proposes $12 million for the Office of Disability Employment Policy (ODEP), returning it to its core mission of policy analysis, technical assistance, and dissemination of effective practices to increase the employment opportunities for people with disabilities. In 2009 ODEP will focus its efforts on developing and implementing disability employment policy to increase the recruitment, retention, and promotion of people with disabilities, and eliminate grant-making activities that are duplicative of activities in other Federal agencies. Staff will also be reduced to reflect the termination of ODEP's grant-making functions.

The Administration remains committed to helping people with disabilities fulfill their full potential. The President outlined this commitment in his New Freedom Initiative in 2002 and the Budget continues to support these ideals, providing a total of $12.5 billion for programs that support the Initiative – an eight percent ($919 million) increase over the 2008 enacted level.

Background

The Congress created ODEP in 2001 to bring a heightened focus within DOL on disability employment through policy evaluation, technical assistance, and development of best practices. ODEP succeeded the expiring President's Task Force on Employment of Adults with Disabilities, which was terminated in 2002 after submitting its final report.

ODEP was tasked with implementing a sustained, coordinated, and aggressive employment strategy to eliminate job barriers for people with disabilities. However, between 2001 and 2005, ODEP expanded its responsibilities to include a $26 million grant program that included homelessness, mental health, international disability, veterans, and homeland security issues—activities that were well beyond ODEP's original mission and duplicative of activities undertaken by other Federal agencies, like the Department of Education and Social Security Administration. A Program Assessment Rating Tool evaluation assessment rated ODEP Results not Demonstrated due to limited performance outcomes and insufficient evaluation data that could help assess the impact and effectiveness of ODEP's policy and coordination efforts.

Department of Labor: Discretionary Proposal
Pilots, Demonstrations, and Research

Funding Summary
(In millions of dollars)

	2008 Enacted	2009 Proposed	Change From 2008
Budget Authority..........................	49	16	-33

Administration Proposal and Impact

The budget for the Department of Labor (DOL) proposes to reduce Workforce Investment Act Pilots, Demonstrations, and Research by $33 million, or 67 percent. The proposed level eliminates unrequested funding that has been added in recent years for numerous narrow-purpose projects that duplicate existing DOL programs and have little accountability for performance outcomes. The Budget also redirects some funding to continue an impact evaluation of the Workforce Investment Act's Adults, Dislocated Worker, and Youth State grant programs.

Background

Section 171(b) of the Workforce Investment Act of 1998 (WIA) authorizes the Secretary of Labor to carry out pilots, demonstrations, and research projects for the purpose of developing and implementing approaches and demonstrating the effectiveness of special methods in addressing training and employment needs. WIA stipulates that grants or contracts awarded for carrying out such projects should be awarded on a competitive basis.

The Congress has traditionally included earmarks and unrequested funding in the WIA Pilots, Demonstrations, and Research activity. The 2008 Consolidated Appropriations Act included over $48 million in funding for earmarks in this activity. Congressional earmarks are awarded without competition and with insufficient accountability for outcomes. Further, the activities funded through the earmarks are not coordinated with existing DOL efforts and often duplicate programs that are supported through the regular WIA State grant programs.

Department of Labor: Discretionary Proposal
Senior Community Service Employment Program

Funding Summary
(In millions of dollars)

	2008 Enacted	2009 Proposed	Change From 2008
Budget Authority.........................	522	350	-172

Administration Proposal and Impact

The Budget proposes $350 million for the Senior Community Service Employment Program (SCSEP), the same as the 2008 Budget but $172 million (33 percent) below the 2008 enacted level. This program was rated Ineffective by the Performance Assessment Rating Tool, largely due to inadequate competition in the grants process, lack of data on program performance and impact, and duplication with other federal programs. The Budget reduces funding for SCSEP, which will support approximately 71,795 participants in 2009, and redirects dollars to other higher priority and more effective programs.

While the Older Americans Act Amendments of 2006 (P.L. 109-365) reauthorized and made some improvements in this program, the program still suffers from inadequate competition and low levels of performance in getting participants into unsubsidized employment. The Department of Labor (DOL) conducted a one-time competition of its national grants (which represent a little more than three-quarters of program funding) in 2006, but the Older Americans Act Amendments prohibited competition beyond the current pool of national grantees until 2010. In program year 2006 (the most recent year for which data are available), the program fell short of its targets for placement in employment, placing less than one-third in unsubsidized jobs.

Background

SCSEP distributes grants to states and public and private non-profit organizations to provide part-time work experience in community service activities to unemployed low-income persons ages 55 and over to perform community service. In 2009, DOL will continue to increase the program's focus on training and employment-related services, and collect data that measures participants' employment, job retention, and earnings outcomes.

Department of Transportation: Discretionary Proposal
Amtrak

Funding Summary
(In millions of dollars)

	2008 Enacted	2009 Proposed	Change From 2008
Budget Authority..........................	1,355	900	-455

Administration Proposal and Impact

The Budget requests $900 million for intercity passenger rail, largely for Amtrak, which is $455 million less than the 2008 enacted level. The 2009 request is part of a multiyear effort by the Administration to reduce, and eventually eliminate, Amtrak's reliance on Federal operating assistance. This reflects the long-standing Administration principle to create an intercity passenger system driven by sound economics. Of the $900 million request, $800 million is for Amtrak directly, including $275 million for operating costs. That amount would set a tight 2009 operating budget, and to curb its losses Amtrak would have to make some hard but needed choices about which services to provide. The Budget seeks $525 million for Amtrak's capital budget, which would support ongoing infrastructure maintenance work including projects along the Northeast Corridor between Washington, D.C. and Boston. The Budget also requests $100 million for capital matching grants to States for intercity passenger rail projects. These funds will enable States and localities, rather than Amtrak, to direct capital investment and address their transportation goals.

Background

Amtrak is the federally-subsidized monopoly provider intercity passenger rail service. Created in 1971, it connects all but four States, and in 2007 it carried 26 million riders. The Administration has sought to reform the railroad because it has consistently suffered major financial losses, provided inferior service, and failed to prioritize its limited resources. For example, the Government Accountability Office has concluded that Amtrak's long-distance trains, which lost $440 million in 2007, "show limited public benefits for dollars expended," and that, "these routes account for 15 percent of riders but 80 percent of financial losses." These same long distance trains had an on-time performance rate of 42 percent in 2007. The 2007 Budget presents an assessment of Amtrak's performance that found that Amtrak's purpose is ambiguous and that its flawed design contributes to its poor performance.

Department of Transportation: Discretionary Proposal
Essential Air Service

Funding Summary
(In millions of dollars)

	2008 Enacted	2009 Proposed	Change From 2008
Budget Authority......................	60*	---*	-60

*Does not include a mandatory $50 million appropriation for this program from overflight fees. The Administration is proposing to continue the $50 million mandatory appropriation in 2008, which is sufficient to fund Essential Air Service to the neediest and most-isolated communities.

Administration Proposal and Impact

The Essential Air Service (EAS) is statutorily funded by a mandatory appropriation of $50 million from overflight fees that has historically been supplemented with a discretionary general fund appropriation. The Budget proposes no discretionary appropriation for this program, along with other reforms. The $50 million is sufficient to subsidize air service to communities to maintain transportation connectivity for the most isolated communities. The Budget proposes revising the criteria to limit eligibility for EAS subsidies to those communities that need them. At the proposed funding level, about half of the currently subsidized communities would still receive service, including those remote places without ready road access to a medium or large hub airport.

Background

The EAS program was established concomitant with airline deregulation in 1978 to mitigate anticipated service reductions at small rural airports resulting from deregulation. For airports with scheduled service prior to 1978, and meeting certain other standards of eligibility based on distance from other airports, EAS subsidizes flights from that airport to a larger airport. Originally anticipated to last for 10 years, the program was first extended for an additional 10 years, and then made permanent.

EAS, however, has been made obsolete over time, particularly by the growth in surface transportation. Consumers in many rural areas now regularly travel the distances required to take advantage of shopping and other services in larger, relatively nearby urban areas, including air transportation services. In some cases, EAS-subsidized flights are averaging less than three passengers at a time, as consumers opt for the price and convenience of ground travel to the nearest large airport, rather than using the EAS-subsidized flight. The program assessment conducted by the Department of Transportation and the Office of Management and Budget showed the program did not use annual and long-term goals to manage the program and it received a rating of Results not Demonstrated.

Department of Transportation: Discretionary Proposal
Federal-Aid Highways

Funding Summary
(In millions of dollars)

	2008 Enacted	2009 Authorized	2009 Proposed	Change from 2009 Authorized	Change From 2008 Enacted
Obligation Limitation............	41,216	40,199	39,399	-800	-1,817

Administration Proposal and Impact

The Budget proposes to reduce the obligation limitation for the Federal Highway Administration's Federal-Aid Highways program. The program provides Federal grants to States for building, operating, maintaining, and managing the Federal highway system. The proposed obligation limitation for Federal-Aid Highways for 2009 includes a reduction that will help place highway spending on a path toward solvency while ensuring that total funding for SAFETEA-LU fulfills the original guarantee of $286.4 billion for surface transportation programs.

Background

SAFTEA-LU, enacted in 2005, provided funding of $286.4 billion for all surface transportation programs, including Federal-Aid Highways, through 2009. In several years since 2005, changes to surface transportation funding – mainly within highway programs – have increased funding by several hundred million above that level. Spending from the Federal-Aid Highways, a program that provides grants to States for construction, maintenance, and management of the Federal highway system, has been by far the largest contributor to an anticipated cash shortfall in the Highway Account of the Highway Trust Fund.

The Budget proposes an obligation limitation for Federal-Aid Highways that conforms to the total level agreed upon for SAFETEA-LU. While the Budget proposes temporary authority for the Highway Account to relieve its cash shortfall during 2009, the Administration proposes that no additional spending authority in excess of what is needed to satisfy the aggregate SAFETA-LU authorization should be provided in 2009, so as not to exacerbate the cash shortfall.

Department of Transportation: Discretionary Proposal
Railroad Rehabilitation and Improvement Financing (RRIF) Loan Program

Funding Summary
(In millions of dollars)

	2008 Enacted	2009 Proposed	Change From 2008
Budget Authority.........................	NA	NA	NA

Administration Proposal and Impact

The Budget again calls for reforming the RRIF program with the aim of better defining the program's purpose. Last year, the Administration transmitted authorizing language to the Congress that would target RRIF program assistance to small railroads in need of government support. It also clarified that the program's goal is to complement lending by the private sector. The proposal would limit the size of RRIF loans to $250 million and limit refinancing of outstanding debt to $50 million. The Budget itself recommends an annual loan limitation of $700 million for 2009, reflecting a more realistic level of demand for credit assistance from small railroads. Moreover, DOT plans to work with the private lending community to develop new opportunities for railroads to obtain private credit including promoting private loans guaranteed by the RRIF program.

Background

The RRIF program, created in 1998, offers low-cost loans to railroads for infrastructure improvement projects or refinancing debt. The latest highway reauthorization bill, SAFETEA-LU, substantially expanded the scope of the program and increased its size from $3.5 billion to $35 billion. In previous budgets, the Administration recommended terminating the program because it lacks a clear purpose and an adequate justification for subsidizing private rail companies. According to the law, project eligibility is virtually open-ended and there are few limits on which companies may apply. Consequently, instead of assisting struggling small railroads as the program was first envisioned, DOT has provided RRIF loans to a range of applicants, some of which have substantial projected revenues.

RRIF is a zero subsidy loan program meaning it does not receive appropriated funds to make loans. However, the program exposes the government to the risk of loan defaults, which is captured in the annual credit subsidy reestimate process.

Environmental Protection Agency: Discretionary Proposal
Clean Water State Revolving Fund

Funding Summary
(In millions of dollars)

	2008 Enacted	2009 Proposed	Change From 2008
Budget Authority..........................	689	555	-134

Administration Proposal and Impact

The Budget funds the Clean Water State Revolving Fund (SRF) at $555 million. From 2004 through 2007 the Congress provided significantly more for the Clean Water SRF than requested (in 2008 the Congress provided the Budget-request level). In view of these increases, the program needs less funding than in previous years to meet the Administration's 2004 Federal funding target of $6.8 billion total for 2004-2011. The proposed funding will enable the Clean Water SRF to provide $3.4 billion in loans annually, even after Federal assistance ends.

Background

The Congress created the Clean Water SRF in 1987 to serve as a long-term funding source for wastewater infrastructure. The Clean Water SRF provides grants to States to capitalize their own wastewater State revolving funds. States provide a 20 percent match and loan Clean Water SRF monies to communities at below-market rates, with loan repayments and interest recycled back into the program, allowing it to "revolve" and finance activities even once Federal funding ends as the legislation intended. Since 1987, EPA has provided approximately $25 billion to help fund the State-run programs. In combination with State monies, bond proceeds, and recycled loan repayments, the Clean Water SRFs have been able to leverage the Federal investment into $61 billion for wastewater infrastructure projects. A Program Assessment Rating Tool review found the program was Adequate.

In recognition of the continued demand for wastewater infrastructure financing, the Budget includes a proposal to exempt water infrastructure private activity bonds (PABs) from the State volume cap. To ensure the proposal advances Administration policies of full-cost pricing and self-sufficiency, the initiative includes a requirement that any entity using the PABs must implement full-cost pricing within five years. The 2008 Budget also included this initiative.

Environmental Protection Agency: Discretionary Proposal
Mexico Border

Funding Summary
(In millions of dollars)

	2008 Enacted	2009 Proposed	Change From 2008
Budget Authority.........................	20	10	-10

Administration Proposal and Impact

The Budget proposes to reduce Mexico Border Infrastructure Assistance funding for water infrastructure projects in the U.S.-Mexico border region. A Program Assessment Rating Tool evaluation identified the need to improve project completion rates to reduce $320 million in unobligated balances. In 2005 EPA implemented new management controls to address this problem; and, as of October 2007 approximately $230 million in unobligated funds were not disbursed. Currently approved construction projects for this program can be completed utilizing the requested funding and the remaining unobligated balances.

Background

The Mexico Border Infrastructure Assistance program is one of the components of the Border 2012 Program. The Border 2012 Program was established in 2002 as a result of the signing of the 1983 "Agreement on Cooperation for the Protection and Improvement of the Environment in the Border Area," also known as the La Paz Agreement. One objective of the Border 2012 Program is to provide access to drinking water to reduce health risks to residents as well as basic sanitation services with the goal of restoring the quality of impaired transboundary surface waters in the border region. The Mexico Border Infrastructure Assistance program fulfills this objective by providing grants for the planning, design and construction of high priority drinking water and wastewater treatment projects in the ten U.S. and Mexican Border States.
The enacted funding for this program was reduced from $49 million in 2007 to $20 million in the 2008 Budget. This 59 percent reduction reflects widespread acknowledgement that new appropriations for this program should be reduced until unobligated balances are reduced.

Environmental Protection Agency: Discretionary Proposal
Nonpoint Source (Sec. 319) Grants

Funding Summary
(In millions of dollars)

	2008 Enacted	2009 Proposed	Change From 2008
Budget Authority........................	201	185	-16

Administration Proposal and Impact

The Budget proposes $185 million for the Environmental Protection Agency's (EPA's) Nonpoint Source (Sec. 319) Grants program. This program is one of EPA's larger categorical grant programs but is not as high a priority as some of the other categorical grants that EPA provides to States to carry out their environmental responsibilities.

While nonpoint source pollution remains a problem nationwide, this program does not generally help States address their core Clean Water Act requirements. Additionally, there are other significant sources of Federal nonpoint source funding available through USDA conservation programs. Other EPA programs like the National Estuary Program and Federal wetland mitigation and restoration programs also can help address nonpoint source pollution.

Background

This program provides grants to States to develop and implement nonpoint source management plans. Nonpoint source pollution is caused by rainfall or snowmelt runoff picking up and carrying pollutants such as fertilizers, oil, and sediment into waterbodies. Typical nonpoint source management projects include buffer strips, stormwater management, and wetlands restoration. A Program Assessment Rating Tool review found the program Adequate.

National Aeronautics and Space Administration: Discretionary Proposal Aeronautics Program

Funding Summary
(In millions of dollars)

	2008 Enacted	2009 Proposed	Change From 2008
Budget Authority.........................	627	545	-82

Administration Proposal and Impact

The Budget proposes to reduce NASA's Aeronautics Program as part of a multiyear effort to focus the program on long-range research in fundamental aeronautics, aviation safety, and air traffic management of broad benefit to the Nation. In the past, the program supported costly demonstration projects with near-term goals that benefited narrow segments of the aeronautics community. This change has achieved savings which have been shifted to other higher priority activities.

Background

Since 1915, NASA's aeronautics program has conducted research to improve the safety and performance of air vehicles and the aviation system. The 2006 Budget proposed restructuring NASA's Aeronautics Program and reducing its budget. In the last three years, the Congress has reduced the aeronautics budget, but to a lesser degree than requested. The 2008 enacted level, for example, was $74 million above the level requested in the 2008 Budget. In the 2009 Budget, these funds are being directed to support other priorities, including the Administration's top priority for NASA, the President's Vision for Space Exploration, a sustained and affordable human and robotic program to explore the solar system.

National Aeronautics and Space Administration: Discretionary Proposal
New Millennium Program

Funding Summary
(In millions of dollars)

	2008 Enacted	2009 Proposed	Change From 2008
Budget Authority...............	58	4	-54

Administration Proposal and Impact

The Budget proposes to reduce NASA's New Millennium Program with the intent of phasing it out in 2011. While the program has advanced many space and Earth science research mission technologies, few of these technologies have been incorporated into NASA space flight missions. NASA will pursue technology advancement in support of future space and Earth science research missions through a variety of other approaches that will ensure that new technologies are more closely tied to mission requirements. The Budget proposes to cancel funding for this program and to redirect the dollars to other higher priority programs.

Background

The goal of the New Millennium Program is to reduce the risks to as well as the costs of future NASA space and Earth science research missions. The program tests certain technologies on independent flights in space before flying them on science research missions in an effort to validate the technologies and reduce technical risk to research missions. The program was established in 1995.

While the program has validated several technologies since its inception, only a few of the technologies advanced through the program have actually flown on NASA missions, indicating that the program may not be the most effective use of technology funds. NASA currently develops technologies to support future research missions through a variety of other approaches that the agency will continue to pursue.

Small Business Administration: Discretionary Proposal
Microloan Program

Funding Summary
(In millions of dollars)

	2008 Enacted	2009 Proposed	Change From 2008
Budget Authority..........................	17	---	-17

Administration Proposal and Impact

The Budget proposes to eliminate direct loan subsidy cost and technical assistance funding for the Small Business Administration (SBA) Microloan program and to operate the program at no cost to the taxpayer. This builds upon the significant success of similar changes made in recent years to SBA's 7(a) guaranteed loan program. With modest reforms, the Microloan program can operate in a more cost-effective manner and without a need for appropriations.

Background

The Microloan program provides small loans to businesses through intermediaries, which also receive SBA technical assistance. Under this program, SBA makes funds available to nonprofit community-based lenders (intermediaries) that, in turn, make loans to eligible borrowers up to a maximum of $35,000.

Considering both loan subsidy and technical assistance, the program costs taxpayers nearly 88 cents for every dollar lent. Taxpayer-funded credit subsidy costs can be eliminated with only marginally increased (but still below-market) interest rates charged to loan intermediaries. Further, intermediaries can absorb technical assistance costs, given existing interest rate formulas and funding from other sources.

Other Agencies: Discretionary Proposal
Corporation for Public Broadcasting

Funding Summary
(In millions of dollars)

	2008 Enacted	2009 Proposed	Change From 2008
Budget Authority........................	448	200	-248

Administration Proposal and Impact

The Budget proposes that the Corporation for Public Broadcasting (CPB) be funded at $200 million, and that non-Federal funding of the public broadcasting system be emphasized going forward. This proposal is consistent with the evolving role of public broadcasting in a market that has benefited from tremendous growth and diversity of programming. The appropriation to the CPB represents only 15 percent of public broadcasting revenue; individual, corporate and foundation donations comprise most of the system's funding.

Background

Programming diversity and consumer choice have grown substantially since CPB was created in 1967, with 86 percent of U.S. households now subscribing to satellite or cable services that provide dozens of channels, including news, cultural, science and other programming. The Administration's proposal is consistent with public broadcasting's changing role.

The Congress has provided CPB advance appropriations for two fiscal years ahead of the typical budget cycle. The Administration has proposed that this practice be discontinued and CPB receive regular budget-year funding.

Other Agencies: Discretionary Proposal
Delta Regional Authority

Funding Summary
(In millions of dollars)

	2008 Enacted	2009 Proposed	Change From 2008
Budget Authority.........................	12	6	-6

Administration Proposal and Impact

The Budget requests $6 million for the Delta Regional Authority, which will reduce the Authority's direct grant-making, but which will allow it to continue its role as a regional planner and coordinator of other Federal investments in the Mississippi Delta region. This area of the country will continue to receive substantial funding for economic development, health care, and job training from other Federal sources such as the Departments of Agriculture, Health and Human Services, Housing and Urban Development, and Labor.

Background

Created in 2000, the Delta Regional Authority was established as a Federal-State partnership to assist the Mississippi Delta region in obtaining transportation, basic public infrastructure, and skill training to enhance regional economic development. In its 2006 Program Assessment Rating Tool reassessment, the Delta Regional Authority was rated as Results Not Demonstrated, due to its lack of annual performance measures and independent program evaluations.

Other Agencies: Discretionary Proposal
Denali Commission

Funding Summary
(In millions of dollars)

	2008 Enacted	2009 Proposed	Change From 2008
Budget Authority..........................	26	6	-20

Administration Proposal and Impact

The Budget requests $6 million for the Denali Commission, which will largely diminish the Commission's direct grant-making, but will allow it to continue its constructive role as a regional planner and coordinator of other Federal investments in Alaska. Alaska will continue to receive funding for economic development, health care, and job training from other Federal sources, and the Denali Commission will assist distressed communities and Federal agencies in developing and carrying out development projects and strategies.

Background

The Denali Commission is a Federal partnership with Alaska to fund utilities, infrastructure, and other assistance to distressed rural communities in the State. While Alaska faces some unique development challenges, the Commission's grant-making is duplicative of other Federal investments in the state. Community and economic development, infrastructure development, and training activities are also supported by several other Federal agencies, including the Departments of Agriculture, Commerce, Health and Human Services, Housing and Urban Development, Labor, and Transportation. In addition, the Program Assessment Rating Tool assessment of the Commission found that it has challenges evaluating the performance and results achieved with its funds. While the Commission has established long term performance goals, the extent to which its investments are having an impact on economic development in rural Alaska is unclear.

National Archives and Records Administration: Discretionary Proposal
National Historical Publications and Records Commission

Funding Summary
(In millions of dollars)

	2008 Enacted	2009 Proposed	Change From 2008
Budget Authority........................	10	---	-10

Administration Proposal and Impact

The Budget proposes no new funding for grants for the National Historical Publications and Records Commission (NHPRC) in order to focus funding on the National Archives and Records Administration's core mission of managing Federal records. The Commission itself would retain all other authorized functions, such as its advisory roles and administration of outstanding grants.

Background

The NHPRC provides grants to States, local governments, universities, and other institutions for projects to preserve and publish non-Federal records. Other Federal agencies, such as the National Endowment for the Humanities, also provide grants for which many NHPRC recipients would be eligible to apply. Finally, several NHPRC projects, such as efforts to publish the papers of the Founding Fathers, have not produced adequate progress, despite being funded for several decades.

Mandatory Savings

Mandatory Program Reforms

(Outlays in millions of dollars)

	2009	2010	2011	2012	2013	2009-13	2009-18
Mandatory Proposals, including Savings and *Augmentations*[1]:							
Agriculture:							
Reauthorize Farm Bill...	*109*	*620*	*790*	*895*	*115*	*2,529*	*2,406*
Charge Food Safety and Inspection Service user fees[2]...	-96	-98	-100	-102	-104	-500	-1,053
Charge Grain Inspection, Packers and Stockyards Administration user fees[2]...	-27	-30	-30	-31	-32	-150	-318
Charge crop insurance user fees[2]...	--	-15	-15	-15	-15	-60	-135
Charge Animal Welfare Act user fees[2]...	-20	-27	-27	-28	-29	-131	-290
Implement country of origin labeling audit program:							
Receipts...	*-10*	*-10*	*-10*	*-10*	*-10*	*-50*	*-100*
Spending...	*10*	*10*	*10*	*10*	*10*	*50*	*100*
Net effect...	*--*	*--*	*--*	*--*	*--*	*--*	*--*
Extend Forest County Safety Net Payments...	*--*	*100*	*60*	*40*	*--*	*200*	*200*
Total, Agriculture...	-34	550	678	759	-65	1,888	810
Education:							
Reform the Federal student aid programs:							
Restrict loans eligible for public sector loan forgiveness...	-1,387	-29	-21	-16	-11	-1,464	-1,485
Eliminate the interest subsidy on loans eligible for income-based repayment...	-260	-47	-45	-48	-56	-457	-788
Recall Perkins Loan balances...	-1,116	-698	-735	-821	-792	-4,162	-7,220
Total, Education...	-2,763	-775	-801	-885	-859	-6,083	-9,493
Energy:							
Repeal oil and gas research and development program...	-20	-40	-50	-50	-50	-210	-300
Health and Human Services:							
Reform Medicare...	-12,437	-26,875	-39,798	-45,741	-53,384	-178,235	-556,373
Reform Medicaid...	-1,767	-2,924	-3,758	-4,305	-4,671	-17,425	-46,748
Reauthorize State Children's Health Insurance Program[3]...	*2,260*	*3,005*	*4,010*	*4,680*	*5,315*	*19,270*	*50,000*
Fund high-risk health insurance pools...	*50*	*75*	*25*	*--*	*--*	*150*	*150*
Eliminate Social Services Block Grant (SSBG)...	--	-1,445	-1,683	-1,700	-1,700	-6,528	-15,028
Provide Temporary Assistance for Needy Families (TANF) supplemental grants and contingency fund for child welfare option...	*236*	*299*	*317*	*323*	*326*	*1,501*	*3,102*
Improve child support enforcement collection tools...	6	9	6	1	-1	21	4
Extend Abstinence Education program...	*25*	*43*	*48*	*49*	*50*	*215*	*465*
Introduce Foster Care child welfare program option...	8	6	21	-8	-25	2	-1

Mandatory Program Reforms
(Outlays in millions of dollars)

	2009	2010	2011	2012	2013	2009-13	2009-18
Mandatory Proposals, including Savings and Augmentations [1] :							
Modify Foster Care District of Columbia Federal Medical Assistance Percentage (FMAP) Rate......	6	6	7	6	7	32	69
Charge Food and Drug Administration re-inspection and export certification fees [2]......	-27	-28	-28	-29	-30	-142	-302
Total, Health and Human Services......	-11,640	-27,829	-40,833	-46,725	-54,113	-181,139	-564,662
Homeland Security:							
Propose a surcharge on the passenger security fee to fund baggage screening systems......	-106	-21	-8	1	107	-29	0
Housing and Urban Development:							
Charge Government-Sponsored Enterprises oversight fee......	-6	-6	-6	-6	-6	-30	-60
Interior:							
Match National Park Centennial Challenge Fund gift receipts......	20	55	80	100	100	355	855
Authorize Arctic National Wildlife Refuge leasing:							
State of Alaska's share:							
Receipts......	--	-3,502	-2	-503	-3	-4,010	-4,025
Expenditures......	--	3,502	2	503	3	4,010	4,025
Federal share:							
Receipts......	--	-3,502	-2	-503	-3	-4,010	-4,025
Require up-front payment of coal bonus bids......	-385	-676	48	506	225	-282	-8
Return to net receipts sharing for energy minerals......	-54	-64	-53	-46	-52	-269	-559
Repeal Energy Policy Act fee prohibition and mandatory permit funds......	-35	-36	-30	-30	-30	-161	-239
Amend Bureau of Land Management (BLM) Federal land sale authority......	-2	-20	-61	-41	-37	-161	-322
Terminate BLM Range Improvement Fund......	-6	-9	-10	-10	-10	-45	-95
Increase fees for migratory bird hunting and conservation stamps [4]......	10	14	14	14	14	66	136
Recover Pick-Sloan project cost......	-23	-23	-23	-23	-23	-115	-230
Implement a settlement to restore the San Joaquin River......	14	-177	19	19	29	-96	17
Total, Interior......	-461	-4,438	-18	-14	213	-4,718	-4,470
Labor:							
Reform Pension Benefit Guaranty Corporation premiums......	-380	-2,217	-2,093	-2,127	-2,056	-8,873	-18,514
Recover Unemployment Insurance overpayments......	--	-470	-504	-356	-362	-1,692	-3,632

Mandatory Program Reforms

(Outlays in millions of dollars)

	2009	2010	2011	2012	2013	2009-13	2009-18
Mandatory Proposals, including Savings and *Augmentations* [1] :							
Implement foreign labor certification user fees:							
Receipts.................................	-95	-95	-95	-95	-95	-475	-950
Spending................................	95	95	95	95	95	475	950
Net effect.............................	---	---	---	---	---	---	---
Reform Federal Employees Compensation Act	-10	-14	-21	-15	-12	-72	-288
Refinance the Black Lung Disability Trust Fund :							
Black Lung Disability Trust Fund........	2,288	-411	-398	-392	-388	699	-1,201
Interest payments on repayable advances......	-2,288	411	398	392	388	-699	1,201
Net effect.............................	---	---	---	---	---	---	---
Reform Trade Adjustment Assistance.........	6	3	8	1	-3	15	-81
Total, Labor..........................	-384	-2,698	-2,610	-2,497	-2,433	-10,622	-22,515
Transportation:							
Modify financing of the Airport and Airway Trust Fund......	---	---	---	---	---	---	-608
Treasury:							
Improve payment transaction integrity.........	-53	-56	-60	-64	-68	-301	-717
Modernize cash investment practices........	-10	-10	-10	-10	-10	-50	-100
Eliminate the 10-year statute of limitations on							
non-tax debt..........................	-15	-8	-8	-8	-8	-47	-87
Extend the rum carryover for Puerto Rico	102	25	---	---	---	127	127
Total, Treasury.........................	24	-49	-78	-82	-86	-271	-777
Veterans Affairs:							
Adopt third-party insurance co-payment offset [2].	-44	-44	-44	-43	-43	-218	-420
Charge medical care enrollment fees for non-disabled							
higher-income veterans and increase pharmacy							
co-payments to align with other health care plans [2]......	-335	-421	-414	-464	-483	-2,117	-4,796
Total, Veterans Affairs..................	-379	-465	-458	-507	-526	-2,335	-5,216
Army Corps of Engineers:							
Collect additional recreation user fees, lease							
receipts, and contributions:							
Receipts.................................	-9	-17	-17	-17	-17	-77	-162
Spending................................	---	8	17	17	17	59	144
Net effect.............................	-9	-9	---	---	---	-18	-18
Commodity Futures Trading Commission:							
Charge user fees [2]......................	-96	-100	-103	-107	-111	-517	-1,130
Environmental Protection Agency:							
Pesticide Fee Collections: increase or reinstate user							
fees and lift cap on pre-manufacture notice fee [2]......	-52	-56	-55	-55	-45	-263	-502

143

Mandatory Program Reforms

(Outlays in millions of dollars)

	2009	2010	2011	2012	2013	2009-13	2009-18
Mandatory Proposals, including Savings and *Augmentations* [1]:							
Federal Communications Commission (FCC):							
Provide spectrum license fee authority	-150	-300	-300	-400	-450	-1,600	-4,081
Charge Ancillary Terrestrial Component spectrum fee	-60	-100	-125	-125	-125	-535	-1,160
Extend spectrum auction authority	---	---	---	-200	-200	-400	-1,400
Auction domestic satellite spectrum	-100	-100	-75	-20	-15	-310	-343
Eliminate Telecommunications Development Fund	-6	-7	-7	-7	-7	-34	-69
Total, FCC	-316	-507	-507	-752	-797	-2,879	-7,053
Office of Personnel Management (OPM):							
Amend Federal Employee Health Benefits Program statute	-40	-147	-248	-327	-403	-1,165	-3,675
Improve equity and administration of the Federal retirement system	*2*	*3*	*4*	*6*	*7*	*22*	*74*
Replace non-foreign cost of living adjustment with locality pay [4]	*==*	*==*	*==*	*==*	*==*	*==*	*==*
Total, OPM	-38	-144	-244	-321	-396	-1,143	-3,601
Social Security Administration (SSA):							
Extend temporarily length of time-limited Supplemental Security Income eligibility for refugees and asylees	*53*	*47*	*49*	*---*	*---*	*149*	*149*
Mandatory Proposals Resulting in Savings	-19,127	-40,670	-50,495	-57,366	-65,104	-232,763	-676,591
Mandatory Program Augmentations and Cost-neutral Proposals	*2,901*	*4,130*	*5,450*	*6,125*	*5,937*	*24,543*	*57,145*
Total, Mandatory Proposals including Savings and Augmentations	-16,226	-36,540	-45,045	-51,241	-59,167	-208,220	-619,446

[1] Descriptions of mandatory proposals resulting in savings follow in this document. *Augmentations*, shown in italicized non-adds on this table, are described elsewhere in the Budget documents.

[2] If enacted, the Administration would work to classify the receipts as discretionary offsets beginning in 2010.

[3] Represents total cost of SCHIP reauthorization, including SCHIP and Medicaid costs as well as spending resulting from outreach grants.

[4] Affects both receipts and outlays. Only the outlay effect is shown here. For receipt effects, see Table S-7 in the main *Budget* volume.

Department of Agriculture: Mandatory Proposal
Food Stamp Program

Funding Summary
(In millions of dollars)

	2009	2010	2011	2012	2013	2009-13	2009-18
Baseline outlays...................	40,233	40,686	40,865	41,615	42,327	205,726	431,283
Proposed change from current law*.......................	-124	-142	-143	-145	-147	-701	-1,318

* Savings from this proposal are included within proposals for reauthorization of the Farm Bill on the mandatory proposal summary table and Table S-6 in the main *Budget* document.

Administration Proposal and Impact

The 2009 Budget proposes to limit Food Stamp categorical eligibility to households receiving Supplemental Security Income (SSI) or Temporary Assistance for Needy Families (TANF) cash benefits. Households receiving TANF-funded services, but not cash, would no longer be automatically eligible for food stamps, but could apply under regular program rules. This proposal conforms the program's rules to their historical intent, ensuring that Federal assistance is targeted to individuals who are most in need. Only households with income or resources above the program's eligibility requirements would be affected by this proposal.

Background

The Food Stamp program provides eligible, low-income households with a voucher in the form of an electronic debit card redeemable for food at retail stores. Eligibility is based on income, expenses, assets and non-financial factors such as citizenship or legal immigration status and fulfillment of applicable work requirements.

Historically, households which were determined eligible for comparable means-tested benefits were deemed "categorically," or automatically, eligible for food stamps. When the TANF program was established, categorical food stamp eligibility was extended to households receiving only TANF-funded services as well as those receiving TANF cash assistance. However, in practice, TANF-funded services are extremely diverse, and do not necessarily have eligibility criteria that are comparable to the Food Stamp program. In some cases, States have expanded categorical eligibility for food stamps to those who have received a pamphlet published with TANF funds. As a result, in some States, households with income and resources above the regular eligibility criteria are able to receive food stamps.

Department of Agriculture: Mandatory Proposal
Food Safety and Inspection Service User Fees

Funding Summary
(In millions of dollars)

	2009	2010	2011	2012	2013	2009-13	2009-18
Proposed change from current law..........................	-96	-98	-100	-102	-104	-500	-1,053

Administration Proposal and Impact

The 2009 Budget proposes two new user fees, a licensing fee and a performance fee. These proposals shift funding for food safety inspection from the general public to the slaughter and processing plants that directly benefit from federal inspection. These two fees are different than those proposed in recent budgets and would offset only a portion of the Food Safety and Inspection Services (FSIS) operational expenses. The recommended fees, saving $96 million in the first year, include:

- $92 million in receipts from a licensing fee scaled to the size of the operation. This fee comes to less than one-tenth of one cent per pound of meat and poultry.
- $4 million for a performance fee. Plants that have resampling and retesting due to positive samples, recalls, or are linked to outbreaks, would pay a fee to FSIS for each incident.

Background
The primary objectives of the Food Safety and Inspection Service (FSIS) are to ensure that meat, poultry, and processed egg products are wholesome, unadulterated, and properly labeled and packaged.

Though the Congress has not been supportive of food safety user fees in the past, FSIS provides a significant benefit to the meat and poultry industry that is appropriately paid for by the industry that benefits. The proposed fee does not try to pass the entire cost of inspection onto the industry and should not be burdensome. In addition, the performance fee is only charged to those that increase the work of FSIS because of poor performance.

The 2004 and 2005 Budgets included discretionary legislative proposals to authorize a new overtime user fee that were not adopted. The 2006 and 2007 Budgets proposed permanent legislation to collect mandatory receipts that also were not adopted. The 2008 Budget included the same proposal as is included in the 2009 Budget, but it was not adopted.

Department of Agriculture: Mandatory Proposal
Grain Inspection, Packers and Stockyards Administration User Fees

Funding Summary
(In millions of dollars)

	2009	2010	2011	2012	2013	2009-13	2009-18
Proposed change from current law........................	-27	-30	-30	-31	-32	-150	-318

Administration Proposal and Impact

The Budget proposes to charge user fees to recover the cost of administering two programs under the Grain Inspection, Packers and Stockyards Administration (GIPSA). These proposals would enable GIPSA to charge fees for: 1) the development, review, and maintenance of official U.S. grain standards; 2) licensing livestock market agents, dealers, stockyards, packers, and swine contractors. Under current law, GIPSA has the authority to prescribe a fee for registration requirements for market agents and dealers, but lacks the authority to retain the fee. In addition, the agency also lacks the authority to assess licensing fees. Both of these proposals shift funding for programs that benefit only specific groups to user fees paid by those groups, instead of relying on general taxpayer-provided funds.

Background

GIPSA's core function is to facilitate the marketing of livestock, poultry, meat, cereals, oilseeds and other related agricultural products and to promote fair and competitive trading practices for the overall benefit of consumers and agricultural producers. GIPSA develops, reviews, and maintains official U.S. grain standards used by the entire grain industry. In addition, GIPSA administers the Packers and Stockyards Act which prohibits deceptive and fraudulent trading practices by livestock market agencies, dealers, stockyards, packers, and swine contractors.

Department of Agriculture: Mandatory Proposal
Crop Insurance User Fee (Risk Management Agency)

Funding Summary
(In millions of dollars)

	2009	2010	2011	2012	2013	2009-13	2009-18
Proposed change from current law.........................	---	-15	-15	-15	-15	-60	-135

Administration Proposal and Impact

The 2009 Budget includes a proposal to implement a participation fee in the Federal crop insurance program. The proposed participation fee would initially be used to fund modernization of the existing information technology (IT) system and would supplement the annual appropriations. Subsequently, the funds resulting from the fee would be shifted to support maintenance activities and would be expected to reduce the annual appropriation. The participation fee would be charged to insurance companies participating in the Federal crop insurance program, based on a rate of about one-half cent per dollar of premium sold. The fee is expected to be sufficient to generate about $15 million annually beginning in 2010.

Background

Subsidized Federal crop insurance administered by the Department of Agriculture's (USDA's) Risk Management Agency (RMA) assists farmers in managing yield and revenue shortfalls due to bad weather or other natural disasters. The USDA crop insurance program is a cooperative effort between the Federal Government and the private insurance industry. Private insurance companies sell and service crop insurance policies. These companies rely on reinsurance provided by the Federal Government and also by the commercial reinsurance market to manage their individual risk portfolio. The Federal Government reimburses private companies for the administrative expenses associated with providing crop insurance and reinsures the private companies for excess insurance losses on all policies. The Federal Government also subsidizes premiums for farmers.

The existing IT system is nearing the end of its useful life and recent years have seen increases in "down-time" resulting from system failures. Over the years, numerous changes have occurred in the Federal crop insurance program, including, the development of revenue and livestock insurance, which have greatly expanded the program and taxed the IT system due to new requirements, such as daily pricing, which were not envisioned when the existing IT system was designed. This has contributed to increased maintenance costs and limited RMA's ability to comply with congressional mandates pertaining to data reconciliation with the Farm Service Agency. The participation fee will alleviate these problems.

Department of Agriculture: Mandatory Proposal
Animal and Plant Health Inspection Service User Fees

Funding Summary
(In millions of dollars)

	2009	2010	2011	2012	2013	2009-13	2009-18
Proposed change from current law........................	-20	-27	-27	-28	-29	-131	-290

Administration Proposal and Impact

The 2009 Budget proposes a user fee to fund the cost of animal welfare inspections for animal research facilities, carriers, and in-transit handlers of animals. In addition, the Budget proposes to charge individuals or companies for licenses to market a veterinary biologic and for permits for biotechnologically derived products. This proposal shifts the source of funding from the general taxpayer to specific groups benefiting from the service.

Background

These programs are operated by the Animal and Plant Health Inspection Service (APHIS). APHIS is responsible for the humane treatment of animals covered by the Animal Welfare Act. The program monitors the humane treatment of animals through inspections of research facilities, certain animal dealers, circuses, and carriers and interstate handlers of animals including the inspection of premises. The fee for veterinary biologics would pay for the review of products for safety, efficacy, and effect. The fee for biotechnology would pay for inspections of biotechnologically derived products during and after the growing season.

The animal welfare fee proposal has been made in the past, but has not been acted on by the Congress. The fee proposals for veterinary biologics and for biotechnology are being proposed for the first time this year.

Department of Education: Mandatory Proposal
Federal Student Loan Reforms

Funding Summary
(In millions of dollars)

	2009	2010	2011	2012	2013	2009-13	2009-18
Baseline outlays	1,392	2,318	2,866	3,041	2,958	12,575	18,007
Proposed change from current law:							
Restrict Loans Eligible for Public Sector Loan Forgiveness	-1,387	-29	-21	-16	-11	-1,464	-1,485
Eliminate the Interest Subsidy on Loans Eligible for Income Based Payment	-260	-47	-45	-48	-56	-457	-788
Eliminate the Perkins Loan Program	-1,116	-698	-735	-821	-792	-4,162	-7,220
Total, Education	-2,763	-775	-801	-885	-859	-6,083	-9,493

Administration Proposal and Impact

The 2009 Budget proposes to amend changes to the student loan programs made by the College Cost Reduction and Access Act (CCRAA). The Administration is making these proposals now so they can be put into effect before the CCRAA changes are fully implemented.

The 2009 Budget's proposals would allow the Department of Education to best target the CCRAA's new benefits to borrowers, ease implementation, and eliminate duplication with other student loan benefits. Specifically, these reforms would:

- Restrict the eligibility for the public service loan forgiveness program created in the CCRAA to new loans beginning in the 2009-2010 academic year;
- Eliminate the three-year interest subsidy on Stafford Loans qualifying for income-based repayment.

The Budget also proposes to eliminate the duplicative Federal Perkins Loan program, and recall the Federal revolving funds from institutions of higher education.

Overall, these student loan proposals will reduce Federal spending by $6.1 billion over five years and $9.5 billion over 10 years.

Background

In 2009, the Federal Government will provide over $95 billion in new grants, loans, and work-study assistance to help students pay for postsecondary education, including $75 billion in student loans and over $18 billion in Pell Grants. Federal student aid can be used to pay for postsecondary education expenses, including tuition, fees, room, and board.

The Department of Education administers two student loan programs with equal terms for students: the Federal Family Education Loan (FFEL) program, a bank-based program where loan capital is provided by private lenders and guaranteed by the Federal Government (begun in 1965), and the William D. Ford Federal Direct Loan Program (DL), a direct lending program where the Federal Government provides the capital (begun in 1994). The Department also manages the Federal Perkins Loan program, where participating institutions make student loans out of Federal revolving funds.

The CCRAA, signed into law in September 2007, made significant changes to Federal student aid programs. However, in doing so it also diverted resources toward poorly targeted policies and new programs, and failed to fully account for their costs. The final bill also failed to resolve implementation issues the Administration raised with some of the bill's changes to the student loan programs.

Background on 2009 Budget Reforms

Public Service Loan Forgiveness. The CCRAA created a new public service loan forgiveness program which permits DL borrowers who work in a broad range of public service positions to have the balance of their loans forgiven after 10 years in repayment. FFEL borrowers must consolidate their loans into DL to qualify for the program.

The 2009 Budget would limit eligibility for this benefit to new borrowers after October 1, 2009. Limiting eligibility to new loans or borrowers is consistent with many prior changes in student loan benefits. The Budget would also target these benefits to those borrowers who have high loan balances and are making initial decisions about their careers – that is, those borrowers who may more strongly consider public service careers because this loan forgiveness is available. Finally, this proposal would also allow time for the student loan marketplace to prepare for potential shifts in loan volume between DL and FFEL.

Income-Based Repayment. The CCRAA created a new loan repayment option in which FFEL and DL borrowers facing "partial economic hardship" can limit their payments to a percentage of their income. For up to three years, the government pays any Stafford Loan interest that accrues and is unpaid under the income-based repayments. Outstanding balances are cancelled after 25 years in repayment.

The 2009 Budget would eliminate the three-year Stafford Loan interest subsidy under this repayment plan. Borrowers with limited income can already access existing economic hardship and unemployment deferments, as well as reduced payment schedules under the new income based repayment.

Federal Perkins Loans. Under the Federal Perkins Loan program, participating institutions of higher education make loans out of Federal revolving funds. A 2003 Program Assessment Rating Tool evaluation found the Perkins Loan program to be Ineffective, as it was duplicative of the larger direct and guaranteed student loan programs and not well-targeted to the neediest students. Under the program statutory formula, most Perkins Loans are offered by institutions with a long history of program participation. Many other institutions that enroll larger numbers of financially needy students receive little or no Perkins Loan funding to offer to these students. The Administration is proposing to eliminate this program and to recall the Federal portion of the Perkins Loans revolving funds currently held by participating institutions. This recall would include both funds held by institutions of higher education at the beginning of the academic year, and subsequent repayments on outstanding Perkins Loans.

Department of Energy: Mandatory Proposal
Oil and Gas Research and Development Programs

Funding Summary
(In millions of dollars)

	2009	2010	2011	2012	2013	2009-13	2009-18
Baseline outlays..................	50	50	50	50	50	250	340
Proposed change from current law.......................	-20	-40	-50	-50	-50	-210	-300

Administration Proposal and Impact

The 2009 Budget proposes to repeal provisions in the 2005 Energy Policy Act for the mandatory oil and gas research and development (R&D) program. These R&D activities typically fund development of technologies that can be commercialized quickly, like improved drill motors. As such, they are more appropriate for the private-sector oil and gas industry to perform, and similar discretionary programs have not demonstrated results, as documented in the Program Assessment Rating Tool review conducted by the Department of Energy and the Office of Management and Budget. The industry has the financial incentives and resources to develop new ways to extract oil and gas from the ground more cheaply and safely. Further, the program has not demonstrated that it is in accord with the Administration's R&D Investment Criteria, which state that programs must demonstrate that industry investment is sub-optimal and avoid duplicating research in areas that are receiving funding from the private sector, especially for evolutionary advances and incremental improvements. The program is operated by a private-sector consortium, so the termination does not impact the Federal workforce.

Background

The Energy Policy Act of 2005 established a new mandatory oil and gas R&D program funded from Federal revenues from oil and gas leases, to be called the Ultra-Deepwater and Unconventional Natural Gas and Other Petroleum Research program. This mandatory program began in 2007. It is similar to the existing discretionary oil and gas R&D programs, also proposed for termination in the 2009 Budget. These programs develop technologies that industry can use to reduce the cost of exploration and production of oil and natural gas reserves. On April 25, 2006, the President said, "these energy companies don't need…the use of taxpayers' money to subsidize…research into deep water drilling."

Department of Health and Human Services: Mandatory Proposal
Medicare

Funding Summary
(In millions of dollars)

	2009	2010	2011	2012	2013	2009-13	2009-18
Baseline outlays....................................	420,077	449,286	494,924	494,712	553,135	2,412,134	5,854,680
Proposed change from current law:							
Encourage and Recognize Competition, Efficiency and Higher Quality Care.......	-7,350	-16,220	-26,470	-30,690	-36,410	-117,140	-383,920
Rationalize Payment Policy.................	-4,800	-9,720	-11,840	-12,880	-13,790	-53,030	-137,550
Improve Program Integrity..................	-250	-960	-1,650	-2,370	-3,290	-8,520	-30,500
Increase Beneficiary Awareness and Responsibility...........................	-460	-820	-1,110	-1,460	-1,900	-5,750	-25,880
Improve Fiscal Sustainability................	---	---	---	---	---	---	---
Premium Interaction (reduced beneficiary premiums due to savings proposals)........	422	845	1,272	1,659	2,006	6,204	21,476
Total*..................................	-12,437	-26,875	-39,798	-45,741	-53,384	-178,235	-556,373

*Reflects savings proposals, net of premium interaction. Savings reflect reductions in payments to Medicare Advantage plans of roughly $43 billion over five years, and $137 billion over 10 years. Does not reflect cost for proposal on qualified individual program.

Administration Proposal and Impact

The 2009 Budget includes proposals to slow the growth in the Medicare program. Over five years, these proposals are estimated to produce a total of $178 billion in net savings for taxpayers and more than $6 billion in premium savings for beneficiaries. Of the net savings amount, $43 billion in savings (nearly one-quarter of total legislative savings) occur in the Medicare Advantage program resulting from the proposed adjustments to provider payments in the traditional fee-for-service Medicare program.

Encourage and Recognize Provider Competition, Efficiency, and Higher Quality Care: Medicare beneficiaries today benefit from innovations that improve their quality of life as they age. These changes in the delivery of care and advances in technology also enhance the health care system by improving productivity and efficiency.

Medicare payments to fee-for-service providers are updated annually by an inflation factor through the market basket update. These updates reflect changes in input prices, and providers benefit from keeping cost growth low. However, current Medicare payment updates do not consider improvements in provider productivity.

The 2009 Budget proposes to modernize the framework for Medicare payment updates to ensure prudent use of taxpayer dollars and encourage quality and efficiency in Medicare providers. The Budget proposes to adjust provider updates for expected productivity gains to recognize and reward providers who strive to achieve efficiencies that restrain costs.

Fee schedules have served as the basis of payment for most items and services covered by Medicare. The Administration seeks to modernize Medicare by increasing competition in the payment to providers for items and services rendered. Enhanced competition encourages and facilitates higher quality of care and lower costs for beneficiaries. Increased competition also creates a more transparent marketplace in the purchase of medical items and services, thereby helping to rationalize the financing of the Medicare program.

The Administration has taken steps to increase competition in Medicare. In 2006, the Administration implemented the new prescription drug benefit, Medicare Part D. Premiums for this benefit are determined by bids submitted by competing drug plans.. In 2007, the Administration began to implement a similar program for the acquisition and payment of durable medical equipment (DME) also covered by the Part B benefit. In addition, Medicare will continue a reform that began in 2006 to introduce competition into the awarding of contracts for beneficiary claims processing, tying contractor payments to accuracy and efficiency of services. While the Medicare Modernization Act (MMA) requires completion of contracting reform by 2011, the Centers for Medicare and Medicaid Services (CMS) is on schedule to complete this reform by 2009. The Medicare baseline assumes mandatory savings estimated at about $2.7 billion from 2009-2013 from contractor reform.

The 2009 Budget proposes to build on Medicare competitive reforms by establishing a national competitive bidding program for clinical laboratory services. Fee schedules, initially established in 1984, currently serve as the basis for payment of clinical laboratory services. Of note, the Inspector General of the Department of Health and Human Services has pointed to the potential for excessive payment and utilization of clinical laboratory services in the Medicare program.

The Budget builds upon the Administration's efforts to improve the quality of care for Medicare beneficiaries through transparency of quality and price information. First, the Budget proposes to build upon existing law by requiring hospitals to report occurrences of "never events" and adjusts payments accordingly. "Never Events" are preventable and serious adverse events (e.g. surgery performed on the wrong body part). Second, the Budget proposes to create a hospital value-based purchasing program that would encourage high-quality care and discourage low-quality care.

The Administration will work to improve efficiency and quality and better target resources in the Quality Improvement Organization (QIO) program, and the Budget includes proposals to enhance competition, performance, and accountability in the program.

The Budget also includes proposals to strengthen regulations for certain hospitals. The proposals would reinstate certain regulations for inpatient rehabilitation hospitals and long-term care hospitals that were modified, deferred, or temporarily rolled back in the Medicare, Medicaid, and SCHIP Extension Act of 2007, P.L. 110-173.

Rationalize Medicare Payment Policy: About one-third of Medicare patients require skilled nursing or rehabilitation care after receiving acute inpatient or outpatient care. These services, referred to as post-acute care (PAC), are paid under the Medicare prospective payment systems (PPS) in four different settings: home health services, skilled nursing facilities (SNF), inpatient rehabilitation facilities (IRF), and long-term care hospitals (LTCH). These divergent payment structures have created a splintered system in which Medicare's payment for similar or identical PAC services vary based on the site of service. They also do not ensure that a patient is sent to the most clinically appropriate and efficient site of care. CMS is implementing a demonstration to collect cost and quality data across PAC settings, which will aid the development of a site-neutral payment system.

The 2009 Budget proposes interim adjustments to payments for IRFs for five conditions involving hip and knee replacements, hip fracture and pulmonary disease. These conditions are commonly treated at both IRFs and SNFs, but cost significantly more when treated in IRFs. For example, based on estimated 2008 average SNF and IRF payments, the average payment to an IRF for unilateral knee replacement equals nearly twice the average payment made to SNFs. The proposal would reduce differences in payment for treatment of the specified conditions to limit inappropriate financial incentives and encourage the provision of care in the most clinically appropriate setting for the beneficiary. IRFs provide intensive inpatient rehabilitation care that may not be needed for patients with relatively uncomplicated conditions whose care needs could reasonably be expected to be met in a SNF.

The Budget includes several policies to improve the value of Medicare spending on beneficiaries. The Budget proposes to streamline and modernize Medicare payments for certain durable medical equipment such as powered wheelchairs and oxygen equipment. These steps will better align rental payments and purchase requirements to more accurately reflect their costs and use, producing savings for taxpayers, the Medicare program, and its beneficiaries.

The Budget proposes to refine several inpatient hospital policies to better align payments with costs and to encourage efficient delivery of health care services. Medicare provides indirect medical education (IME) payments to teaching hospitals, which augment the standard payment to reflect estimated higher costs teaching hospitals may face due to factors such as inefficiencies associated with medical residents' learning or unmeasured differences in the severity of patients' illness. These payments have always been set higher than the estimated effect of teaching on costs per case. The Budget proposes to adjust IME payments to better align them with estimated costs and to phase out a duplicate IME payment to teaching hospitals that is made on behalf of certain beneficiaries.

Medicare also augments payments for certain hospitals that serve a substantial percentage of low-income Medicare and Medicaid patients. Disproportionate share hospital (DSH) payments were originally intended to account for the estimated higher costs of treating low-income patients. However, little relationship exists between care of low-income patients and Medicare costs per case. The Budget proposes to adjust DSH payments to better align them with the estimated cost impact of care to low-income patients.

The 2009 Budget proposes to adjust inpatient hospital capital payments to ensure they are aligned appropriately with costs and to modify how budget neutrality is achieved for certain adjustments to hospital payments for area differences in hospital labor costs.

Medicare pays for certain outpatient dialysis services for beneficiaries with end-stage renal disease (ESRD) based on a system that was initially developed using data from the late 1970s. Since then, treatment has changed with technological advances. In addition, the current system contains incentives for providers to utilize drugs inefficiently, as Medicare pays for certain dialysis drugs according to the number of units given to patients. The Budget proposes to modernize payments for ESRD services to more appropriately reflect costs and encourage efficiencies.

Last, Medicare beneficiaries often have supplemental medical insurance provided through employers. The Medicare Secondary Payer (MSP) program coordinates payment of benefits between private payers and Medicare to determine whether Medicare or the supplemental private insurance should have primary responsibility for payment of a beneficiary's health care claims. Currently, Medicare has secondary payer status for beneficiaries with end-stage renal disease (ESRD) during the first 30 months of care from the onset of the disease regardless of employer size. The 2009 Budget proposes to extend the current 30 month MSP status to five years for ESRD beneficiaries covered by health plans of large employers (100 or more employees). The proposal would not alter current policy for employer health plans covering firms with fewer than 100 employees.

Improve Program Integrity: Medicare seeks to ensure appropriate payment for services rendered. To that end, the Health Care Fraud and Abuse Control (HCFAC) program works to eliminate fraud and abuse within the Medicare program. The Medicare bad debt payment system currently reimburses providers for unpaid beneficiary cost-sharing.

The 2009 Budget proposes to strengthen the integrity of health benefit payments made by the Federal Government. First, the Budget requests $198 million for efforts to protect the Medicare prescription drug benefit and the Medicare Advantage program against fraud, waste, and abuse. These funds are part of a Government-wide Budget proposal to fund program integrity activities through a three-year discretionary cap adjustment.

In addition, the Budget proposes to eliminate Medicare bad debt payment to providers for unpaid beneficiary cost-sharing. The policy would encourage providers to take responsibility for collecting co-payments and deductibles as they do with non-Medicare patients. The Budget also proposes to limit provider ability to challenge adverse Medicare decisions in the courts. This proposal would limit mandamus jurisdiction as a basis for obtaining judicial review, and clarify the Secretary's authority to resolve appeals of Medicare determinations.

Increase Beneficiaries' Awareness of and Responsibility for Their Own Health Care – Part B Premium Subsidies: Medicare beneficiaries voluntarily enroll in Part B, and pay monthly premiums for Part B services, which represent approximately 25 percent of total Part B costs. The Part B benefit covers physicians' services, hospital outpatient services, medical equipment and supplies, ambulatory surgical center services, laboratory tests, and certain other items and services.

As required by the MMA, beginning in 2007 certain higher-income beneficiaries received reduced Part B premium subsidies. In 2008, single beneficiaries with incomes of $82,000 or higher and couples with incomes of $164,000 or higher are receiving reduced premium subsidies on a sliding scale based on income. Thus, while beneficiaries with incomes lower than these thresholds will continue to receive the current 75 percent premium subsidy, the Part B subsidy will be 65 percent for those just above the income thresholds decreasing to 20 percent for single beneficiaries with incomes of $205,000 or more ($410,000 for couples). The reduced subsidies are phased in over three years, as specified by the Deficit Reduction Act of 2006, and the income thresholds are indexed annually to inflation.

The 2009 Budget proposes to cease annually indexing income thresholds when determining eligibility for reduced Medicare Part B premium subsidies. Rather than increasing the income threshold every year by inflation when assessing reduced subsidy eligibility, this proposal slowly increases the number of beneficiaries eligible for reduced subsidies in later years. This proposal encourages awareness of and increases responsibility for health care costs for higher income beneficiaries.

Increase Beneficiaries' Awareness of and Responsibility for Their Own Health Care - Part D Premium Subsidies: Medicare beneficiaries voluntarily enroll in Part D, and pay monthly premiums for Part D benefits, which amount to about 25 percent of Part D costs. The 2009 Budget proposes to similarly income-relate Part D premium subsidies using the current law thresholds applied to the Part B income-related premium subsidies. Like the proposal for Part B premiums, the Budget proposes to not annually index income thresholds when determining beneficiary eligibility for reduced Part D premium subsidies. This proposal fosters increased beneficiary awareness and responsibility for health care costs.

Improve Fiscal Sustainability: Medicare is funded by a dedicated payroll tax (the Hospital Insurance or HI trust fund) and out of general revenues (the Supplementary Medical Insurance or SMI trust fund). Growth in Medicare spending exceeds the rate of inflation, and Medicare is expected to account for approximately 16 percent of total Federal outlays by 2013. The Medicare Trustees estimate that total Medicare expenditures will be almost 3.3 percent of GDP in 2008, climbing to 8.0 percent of GDP in 2040, and reaching more than 11 percent by 2080. The Medicare Trustees estimate that the unfunded liability facing the Medicare program – the gap between its estimated revenue needs and its resources – totals $34 trillion over the next 75 years.

The Administration is committed to slowing Medicare's rate of growth while also promoting the delivery of high-quality care to program beneficiaries. Specifically, the MMA created a "Combined Medicare Trust Fund Analysis" that requires the Trustees to analyze Medicare general revenue funding as a percentage of total Medicare outlays as if the Trust Funds were combined. If the Trustees determine that general revenue funding exceeds a fixed threshold of 45 percent at any time within the current or next six years, they must issue a finding of "excess general revenue Medicare funding". In their 2006 report, the Trustees found that general revenue funding would first reach the 45 percent level in 2012, within the seven-year window. In their 2007 report, the Trustees found that general revenue funding would first reach the 45 percent level in 2013, within the seven-year window. Because this finding has been present in two consecutive Trustees' reports, a "Medicare funding warning" has been triggered. With this trigger, the MMA calls for the President to submit legislation to respond to the funding warning.

The 2009 Budget proposes to strengthen the MMA's solvency provision. If Congress fails to act after the Trustee warnings, the Administration proposes to require a four-tenths of one percent automatic across-the-board cut in Medicare beginning in the year the 45 percent threshold is exceeded. The reduction would grow by increments of four-tenths of one percent in each consecutive year the threshold is exceeded. These reductions would serve as a fail-safe measure, only to be implemented if legislation to address the Trustee warnings is not enacted. Under the Budget's Medicare proposals, the Administration does not expect the 45 percent threshold to be exceeded within the ten-year Budget window (2009-2018). As a result, there are no savings assumed from this proposal within the 5-year (2009-2013) or 10-year (2009-2018) budget window.

Background

The Medicare program, established in 1965, offers health care services to individuals aged 65 and older and certain people with disabilities. Medicare has traditionally consisted of two parts: Hospital Insurance (HI), also known as Part A, and Supplementary Medical Insurance (SMI), also known as Part B. A third part of Medicare, sometimes known as Part C, is the Medicare Advantage program, which expands beneficiaries' options for participation in private-sector health care plans. The MMA established a fourth part of Medicare: a new prescription drug benefit, also known as Part D, which began in 2006. In 2007, nearly 44 million people were enrolled in the Medicare program. As of December 2007, nearly nine million Medicare beneficiaries have chosen to participate in a Medicare Advantage plan. As of January 2008, over 25 million beneficiaries were enrolled in a prescription drug plan.

Department of Health and Human Services: Mandatory Proposal Medicaid

Funding Summary
(In millions of dollars)

	2009	2010	2011	2012	2013	2009-13	2009-18
Baseline outlays	217,537	233,130	250,891	270,284	291,534	1,263,377	3,107,568
Proposed change from current law:							
Medicaid Administrative Service Reforms	-1,230	-1,355	-1,490	-1,555	-1,625	-7,255	-16,585
Medicaid Reimbursement Reforms	-970	-825	-885	-1,095	-1,170	-4,945	-12,205
Medicaid Pharmacy Reforms	-195	-210	-220	-235	-250	-1,110	-2,640
Program Integrity Reforms	-127	-259	-413	-485	-626	-1,910	-6,498
Long Term Care Reforms	-100	-170	-220	-290	-350	-1,130	-3,520
Managed Care Reforms	-100	-300	-500	-600	-600	-2,100	-6,000
Medicaid augmentations	955	195	-30	-45	-50	1,025	700
Subtotal, Medicaid reforms	-1,767	-2,924	-3,758	-4,305	-4,671	-17,425	-46,748
Other Medicaid interactions:							
SCHIP Reauthorization	130	50	25	5	25	235	2,445
Refugee Exemption Extension	32	29	31	---	---	92	92
Net impact	-1,605	-2,845	-3,702	-4,300	-4,646	-17,098	-44,211

Administration Proposal and Impact

Medicaid Administrative Services Reforms

Aligning Medicaid Administrative Reimbursement Rates at 50 Percent: The 2009 Budget proposes to reimburse all administrative activities in Medicaid at 50 percent. While 50 percent is the normal match rate for most administrative costs, there are several exceptions where Federal reimbursement is higher. This proposal would establish consistency in Federal match rates across all administrative activities.

Improve Cost Allocation: The 2009 Budget proposes to reduce duplicate Medicaid payments that were improperly included in Temporary Assistance to Needy Families (TANF) block grants. The 1996 welfare reform law capped Federal funding for administrative costs under TANF and eliminated the open-ended matching structure for administrative costs in Aid to Families with Dependent Children (AFDC). Under the AFDC structure, States generally allocated most of the common eligibility determination costs for AFDC, Medicaid, and Food Stamps to AFDC/TANF. Medicaid's share of these expenses was inappropriately included in the TANF block grant, and as a result, States received a payment windfall. This proposal would correct these duplicate payments by reducing Medicaid administrative funding to account for Medicaid costs that were assumed in the TANF block grant.

Medicaid Reimbursement Reforms

Appropriate Payment for Medicaid Case Management (CM) Services: The 2009 Budget proposes to align the Federal matching rate for case management services with the standard administrative matching rate of 50 percent. Case management is largely an administrative activity; therefore, it is appropriate to reimburse it at 50 percent, similar to other Medicaid administrative activities. Some States have inappropriately classified CM services in order to secure a higher matching rate. This proposal does not affect the amount of reimbursement that States will receive for other Medicaid services to which an individual may be referred by a case manager. This proposal only affects States whose Federal matching rate for medical services is above 50 percent.

Align Family Planning Match Rate: Generally, the Federal Government pays for medical expenses based on each State's statutorily-determined Federal Medical Assistance Percentage (FMAP). However, some medical services are exempt from the formula and are reimbursed at a higher rate. Currently, family planning services are reimbursed at a special match rate of 90 percent. To create consistency and preserve the integrity of the Federal matching structure across medical services, the 2009 Budget proposes to align the Federal matching rate for family planning services to the statutorily-determined FMAP.

Align Qualified Individuals (QI) Program Match Rate: Medicare beneficiaries with incomes between 120 and 135 percent of the Federal Poverty Level, referred to as QIs, are eligible to have their Medicare premiums paid for by Medicaid. This assistance is currently 100 percent federally funded, though other programs for low-income Medicare beneficiaries are reimbursed at the statutorily-determined FMAP formula. To create consistency in reimbursement rates across Medicaid, treat all dually-eligible populations equitably, and preserve the integrity of the matching rates, the 2009 Budget proposes to align QI to the statutorily-determined FMAP formula.

Measuring Medicaid Performance: To improve Medicaid accountability, the 2009 Budget proposes to measure and link Federal grant awards to a State's performance in several areas. States that lag behind in selected performance measures would be given some time to bring their programs up to standard. If a State does not make progress within specified timeframes, then Federal funding would be affected. The proposal encourages States to improve quality, efficiency, and program integrity.

Pharmacy Reform

Rationalizing Pharmacy Reimbursement: In recent years, the Inspector General of the Department of Health and Human Services has found that States overpay pharmacies for prescription drugs. The Deficit Reduction Act (DRA) of 2005 reduced these overpayments by creating a market-price based Federal upper limit (FUL) reimbursement methodology for multiple source drugs. The 2009 Budget proposes building on the FUL calculation changes in the DRA to further reduce these overpayments. The Budget proposes amending the FUL to 150 percent of the average manufacturers price (AMP) for multiple source drugs, adjusted from the 250 percent of AMP as established by the DRA.

Program Integrity Reforms

Extend Asset Verification: The 2009 Budget proposes to extend permanently and make modifications to a web-based asset verification pilot that uses electronic financial records to verify an applicant's assets and eligibility.

Enhance Third-Party Liability: The 2009 Budget proposes three changes that will increase the amount of reimbursement from third parties to States and the Federal Government. The first proposal would amend the statute so that States could only "pay and chase" for prenatal and preventive pediatric services if a third party has not paid within 90 days. After 90 days, States would pay the claim while continuing to seek reimbursement from the third party. The second proposal applies to third-party claims involving medical child support. Current law requires States to "pay and chase" these claims if third-party payment has not been received within 30 days. The Budget proposes to extend this period to 90 days. The third Budget proposal would enhance tort settlement recoveries. This proposal would amend statute to permit States to use liens against all components of liability settlements to recover costs.

Require State Participation in *the Public Assistance Reporting Information System (PARIS):* The 2009 Budget proposes to condition receiving FMAP for Medicaid claims and eligibility systems on participation in PARIS. PARIS is a program that allows States to share eligibility information with each other for a number of public assistance programs, including Medicaid, Food Stamps, and TANF. Using Social Security numbers, States can match lists of beneficiaries to determine whether individuals are receiving benefits in multiple States at the same time.

Mandate National Correct Coding Initiative (NCCI): HHS has developed the NCCI system for Medicare to edit claims submissions to help control improper coding. For example, there are automated edits that examine Medicare claims submissions when providers bill for more than one service for the same beneficiary for the same date of service. The 2009 Budget proposes to require States to include these HHS edits into their claims processing system.

Long Term Care (LTC) Reforms

Maintain LTC Home Equity Amount at $500,000: With some exceptions, the DRA does not permit individuals who have more than $500,000 in home equity to be eligible for LTC services. States have the option to increase the limit to $750,000. The 2009 Budget proposes to remove this option and maintain the limit at $500,000, which is consistent with Medicaid's mission to serve low-income individuals.

Redesign Acute Care Benefits for Higher Income LTC groups: The 2009 Budget proposes to give States the option to redesign acute care services in a more flexible manner for higher income elderly and disabled groups. The proposal builds off of the DRA provision that established a benefit package flexibility option for specific children and adult groups. Selected groups, including children and pregnant women with disabilities, are exempt from this proposal.

Managed Care Reform

Repeal Section 1932(a)(2) Special Rules: Section 1932 of the Social Security Act allows States to use State plan authority to require beneficiaries to enroll in managed care but exempts children with special health care needs, dual eligibles, and Native Americans. To mandate enrollment of any of these populations in managed care, States must submit and gain Federal approval of a waiver. To facilitate managed care expansions for special populations, this proposal would allow States to mandate enrollment of all beneficiaries in managed care through their State plans.

Medicaid Augmentations

The 2009 Budget proposes to continue covering, through September 30, 2009, individuals who qualify for benefits through Transitional Medical Assistance or who qualify for Medicare Part B premium assistance as a Qualified Individual, so that enrollment for current beneficiaries will not be interrupted. The 2009 Budget also proposes to enhance States' abilities to implement premium assistance programs by providing greater flexibility to determine cost effectiveness. This proposal would also provide States with better access to necessary information for determining cost effectiveness by requiring participating employers to share their health plan information with States.

Other Medicaid Interactions

Impact of State Children's Health Insurance Program (SCHIP) Reauthorization

Established in 1997, SCHIP provides health care coverage to low-income, uninsured children who do not qualify for Medicaid. The 2009 Budget proposes to reauthorize SCHIP through 2013. The Budget continues to prioritize low-income children by including allotments to meet anticipated State need in covering low-income uninsured children. To meet this goal, allotments to States would increase by $19.7 billion through 2013. The Budget also includes outreach grants of $50 million in 2009 and $100 million in each of the following four years for States, localities, schools, and community-based organizations to reach eligible, uninsured children.

The reauthorization proposal will ensure SCHIP is preserved to help those who are now uninsured obtain health insurance, but does not move those who now have private health insurance into government programs. The proposal also clarifies SCHIP eligibility by clearly defining income.

The SCHIP reauthorization proposal includes a Medicaid impact that reflects the transition of adults from SCHIP to Medicaid, an increase in Medicaid enrollment due to the outreach grants, and some Medicaid savings associated with more children remaining enrolled in SCHIP.

Impact of Refugee Exemption Extension

This Social Security Administration proposal, which has a Medicaid impact, extends from seven to eight years, the length of time refugees and asylees have to complete the citizenship application process without penalty. This proposal would extend the exemption through FY 2011.

Background

Created in 1965, Medicaid is an open-ended means-tested entitlement program that is jointly financed by the Federal Government and the States. In 2009, Medicaid is projected to provide health coverage and services to nearly 50.8 million low-income children, pregnant women, elderly, and disabled individuals during the year. Medicaid's complexity and open-ended financing structure encourage efforts by States to draw down Federal matching funds, sometimes inappropriately. These financing practices undermine the Federal-State partnership and jeopardize the financial stability of the program. The 2009 Budget proposes to build on past efforts to ensure the fiscal integrity of Medicaid, while still projecting a robust average annual growth rate of more than 7 percent.

Department of Health and Human Services: Mandatory Proposal
Social Services Block Grant

Funding Summary
(In millions of dollars)

	2009	2010	2011	2012	2013	2009-13	2009-18
Baseline outlays..................	1,700	1,700	1,700	1,700	1,700	8,500	17,000
Proposed change from current law........................	---*	-1,445	-1,683	-1,700	-1,700	-6,528	-15,028

* Savings of $500 million in 2009 will be achieved through discretionary appropriations, and are included in the section of this volume devoted to discretionary reforms and reductions.

Administration Proposal and Impact

The Budget proposes to reduce funding for the Social Services Block Grant by $500 million, to $1.2 billion, through appropriations for 2009, and to terminate authorization for SSBG in 2010 and beyond. Federal support for social services will continue through other funding streams that have clearly defined goals and measurable performance objectives. The program lacks performance measures or other means to demonstrate that activities supported by SSBG funds are producing results. SSBG overlaps with other Federal social service programs that serve low-income and needy families including Federal child care and child welfare programs, Temporary Assistance for Needy Families, and programs that provide services to the elderly.

Background

SSBG was established in 1981 to help States provide a broad range of social services to help needy families achieve economic self-sufficiency, to prevent or remedy neglect or abuse, and secure institutional care, when appropriate. States receive a capped block grant with few Federal requirements. While this approach maximizes State flexibility to determine what services to provide and whom to serve, it does not ensure that funds are directed most effectively.

Department of Health and Human Services: Mandatory Proposal Re-inspection and Export Certification Fees

Funding Summary
(In millions of dollars)

	2009	2010	2011	2012	2013	2009-13	2009-18
Proposed change from current law...	-27	-28	-28	-29	-30	-142	-302

Administration Proposal and Impact

The 2009 Budget includes two new Food and Drug Administration (FDA) mandatory user fees that: 1) enable FDA to assess fees for follow-up re-inspections (estimated collections of $23 million) required when violations of Good Manufacturing Practices are found during initial inspections; 2) expand FDA's current authority to collect user fees for issuing export certificates for human drugs, animal drugs and devices to also include food and animal feed (estimated collections of $4 million).

The Administration's proposed user fees will improve the management of FDA's re-inspections of manufacturing facilities and issuance of export certificates. A fee for repeat inspections will serve as an incentive to industry to conform to Good Manufacturing Practices and will more equitably share the financial burden of re-inspections between industry and the public. Expanding the export certification fee to cover food and animal feed brings consistency across all FDA regulated products and eliminates the preferential treatment of the food and feed industry, which currently do not pay for export certificates.

Background

The FDA regulates the safety and effectiveness of human and animal drugs; medical devices, vaccines, and animal feeds; and the safety of food. It accomplishes these tasks through pre-market review of new products and continued safety surveillance of products already available to consumers.

Currently, the FDA charges a variety of user fees for activities such as pre-market review of prescription drugs, animal drugs and medical devices; the issuance of export certificates for human and animal drugs; and medical devices. FDA issues export certificates for some of the products it regulates to attest to the safety of these products. Although FDA issues export certifications for all products it regulates, FDA can only charge a fee to issue export certifications for human and animal drugs, and medical devices. FDA does not have authority to charge a fee for issuing export certificates for food and animal feed.

FDA conducts post-market inspections of food, human drug, biologic, animal drug and feed, and medical device manufacturers (both domestic and foreign) to assess their compliance with Good Manufacturing Practice requirements. Under current law, FDA does not have the authority to assess fees for follow-up inspections required to ensure that manufacturers have addressed violations that were found during the initial inspection.

Department of Housing and Urban Development: Mandatory Proposal
Government-Sponsored Enterprise Oversight Fee

Funding Summary
(In millions of dollars)

	2009	2010	2011	2012	2013	2009-13	2009-18
Proposed change from current law....................................	-6	-6	-6	-6	-6	-30	-60

Administration Proposal and Impact

The President's Budget includes a proposal for a strengthened regulator for the housing Government-Sponsored Enterprises (GSEs) – Fannie Mae, Freddie Mac, and the Federal Home Loan Bank System. As part of this reform, the cost of the regulatory responsibilities of the Department of Housing and Urban Development (HUD) under the Federal Housing Enterprise Safety and Soundness Act of 1992 would be assessed on Fannie Mae and Freddie Mac. The cost of these responsibilities is currently in the HUD salaries and expenses account as a non-reimbursable expense. This mandatory fee would reimburse the Federal Government for the cost of these responsibilities, consistent with the GSEs' current law reimbursement of their Federal safety and soundness regulators' expenses.

Background

HUD's responsibilities regarding GSE oversight include the establishment and enforcement of affordable housing goals for Fannie Mae and Freddie Mac, ensuring their compliance with fair housing laws, and providing consultation to the safety and soundness regulator on GSE activities.

Department of the Interior: Mandatory Proposal
Arctic National Wildlife Refuge Lease Bonuses

Funding Summary
(In millions of dollars)

	2009	2010	2011	2012	2013	2009-13	2009-18
Baseline outlays....................	--	--	--	--	--	--	--
Proposed change from current law........................	---	-3,502	-2	-503	-3	-4,010	-4,025

Administration Proposal and Impact

The 2009 Budget proposes to authorize exploration and environmentally responsible oil and gas development in one of the most promising areas for future domestic oil and gas development, the coastal plain of the Arctic National Wildlife Refuge (ANWR). Technological advances have dramatically reduced the environmental impact of new oil and gas production. As proposed, the development footprint from production in ANWR would cover only about one-tenth of one percent of the coastal plain (also referred to as the "1002 Area").

The State of Alaska would receive half of the revenues from bonus bids, rents, and royalties collected from oil and gas production in ANWR. The 2009 Budget supports the necessary environmental reviews and other required activities to begin ANWR leasing in 2010.

Background

In 1980, the Congress enacted the Alaska National Interest Lands Conservation Act (ANILCA), which redesignated the Arctic Range as ANWR, and expanded its boundaries to include an additional 9.2 million acres. ANILCA designated much of the original Refuge as a wilderness area. However, the Act did not preclude the consideration of resource development on the coastal plain.

Reducing the Nation's dependence on foreign energy sources is a top Administration priority. The Department of the Interior estimates that the 1002 Area holds between 5.7 billion and 16 billion barrels of recoverable reserves, or, at peak production, up to 1 million barrels per day of new domestic oil supply. This daily production is equivalent to nearly 10 percent of our Nation's current daily imports.

Department of the Interior: Mandatory Proposal
Require Up-front Payment of Coal Bonus Bids

Funding Summary
(In millions of dollars)

	2009	2010	2011	2012	2013	2009-13	2009-18
Baseline outlays..................	--	--	--	--	--	--	--
Proposed change from current law........................	-385	-676	48	506	225	-282	-8

Administration Proposal and Impact

The 2009 Budget proposes to amend the Mineral Leasing Act (MLA) to require full bonus bid payments for coal lease sales to be made in the sale year, instead of allowing bonus bid payments to be made over a five-year period.

As a general matter, bidders for coal leases have sufficient resources to pay the full amount of a winning bid up front, and therefore, it is reasonable to provide the same treatment as bidders for other mineral resources (e.g., oil and natural gas) governed by the MLA. This proposal would increase near-term revenues, but would reduce revenues in later years when deferred payments under the current system would otherwise be collected. Fifty percent of coal bonus bid revenues are currently provided to the states, so the proposal would have an identical impact on State revenues.

Background

The Mineral Leasing Act lays out the general requirements for leasing coal on Federal lands and requires, among other things, that the Bureau of Land Management hold regular coal lease sales and that at least 50 percent of coal sale bonus bids be collected under a deferred payment system. The Department of the Interior has enacted regulations to implement the deferred payment system by allowing companies to pay bonus bids over a period of five years.

Department of the Interior: Mandatory Proposal
Return to Net Receipts Sharing for Energy Minerals

Funding Summary
(In millions of dollars)

	2009	2010	2011	2012	2013	2009-13	2009-18
Baseline outlays..................	--	--	--	--	--	--	--
Proposed change from current law........................	-54	-64	-53	-46	-52	-269	-559

Administration Proposal and Impact

In order to partially cover the costs of administering the Federal mineral leasing program, the 2009 Budget proposes to amend the Mineral Leasing Act (MLA) to allow Minerals Management Service (MMS) to deduct two percent from the mineral leasing revenue payments made to States under the 50/50 Federal-State revenue sharing arrangement established by the Act. (This amounts to a reallocation of one percent of the total MLA revenues.)

The Administration's proposal would return to a form of net receipts sharing similar to that which was in place during the 1990s. However, the proposal addresses many of the concerns of critics of the original net receipt sharing process by simplifying how costs are allocated. Instead of attempting to allocate program costs on a State-by-State basis, the Budget proposes a simple two percent deduction from gross receipts prior to making individual State allocations.

It is an appropriate time for establishing a more equitable Federal/State revenue-sharing arrangement because State payments from Federal mineral revenues have increased dramatically in the last few years.

Background

In general, States receive 50 percent of Federal revenues generated from mineral production occurring on Federal lands within that State's boundaries. During most of the 1990s, MMS was authorized to deduct a certain amount from State mineral revenue payments based on an assessment of the Federal Government's costs to manage and oversee mineral leasing and production. This approach was often referred to as "net receipts sharing", or NRS, as it was based on the concept that because States are equal partners in sharing in the revenues from Federal mineral production, they should also share in the costs of managing that production.

In the late 1990s, there was considerable debate about the complex process for assigning costs to a given State and the fairness of the end result. It also became costly and time-consuming for MMS to administer the process. The Mineral Revenue Payments Clarification Act of 2000 (enacted as Title V of the Secure Rural Schools and Community Self-Determination Act, P.L. 106-393) repealed NRS, thereby changing the 50/50 Federal-State revenue sharing arrangement for mineral leasing receipts to provide payments to States from gross revenues (i.e., prior to the Federal agencies deducting their costs of managing the program). This provided States with a windfall because they receive an equal share of the revenues from Federal production, without sharing in the costs of permitting that production.

As part of the 2008 Consolidated Appropriations Act, the Congress effectively implemented the Administration's NRS proposal for one year by requiring a two-percent reduction to state mineral payments for 2008. The Administration continues to seek to implement NRS on a permanent basis through an amendment to the MLA.

Department of the Interior: Mandatory Proposal
Repeal Energy Policy Act Fee Prohibition
and Mandatory Permit Funds

Funding Summary
(In millions of dollars)

	2009	2010	2011	2012	2013	2009-13	2009-18
Baseline outlays..................	--	--	--	--	--	--	--
Proposed change from current law........................	-35	-36	-30	-30	-30	-161	-239

Administration Proposal and Impact

To ensure the Federal Government receives fair compensation for the use of the Nation's land and minerals, the 2009 Budget proposes to repeal a provision in the 2005 Energy Policy Act (EPAct) that prohibits the Bureau of Land Management (BLM) from implementing new user fees for oil and gas permit processing and diverted existing rental receipts to make up for the foregone fee receipts. This proposal would repeal these changes and replace the mandatory funding provided by EPAct with user fees. The proposal would also repeal a mandatory geothermal program fund drawn from Federal geothermal royalties and return to the traditional 50/50 Federal-State revenue sharing arrangement for geothermal revenues.

This proposal supports the Administration's efforts to charge for Government services where the direct beneficiary can be identified. It will shift these costs from taxpayers and allow the Department of the Interior (DOI) to better process permit applications as demand increases. The proposed fees are expected to generate roughly $34 million per year beginning in 2009, thereby reducing the cost to taxpayers for operating a program that benefits specific users. Additional savings will be generated by discontinuing the EPAct mandatory spending provisions related to geothermal receipts.

Background

BLM's Energy and Minerals program is responsible for managing the development of federally owned minerals such as oil, gas, coal, sand and gravel. A 1995 report from DOI's Office of Inspector General found that the program did not adequately charge users of the public lands for specific services performed on behalf of those users. In 2004, the Administration began a new effort to address this shortcoming and institute new fees in the program.

In 2005, BLM was on the verge of implementing a rulemaking to put the new fees in place when EPAct prohibited the agency from doing so. The Act also diverted from the Treasury the Federal share of geothermal leasing revenues; 25 percent of total receipts is now deposited in a BLM geothermal fund and the remaining 25 percent is provided to counties where geothermal production is occurring (in addition to the 50 percent already provided to the States). This is inconsistent with the longstanding 50/50 Federal-State revenue sharing arrangements under the Mineral Leasing Act.

Department of the Interior: Mandatory Proposal
Amend Bureau of Land Management Federal Land Sale Authority

Funding Summary
(In millions of dollars)

	2009	2010	2011	2012	2013	2009-13	2009-18
Baseline outlays....................	--	--	--	--	--	--	--
Proposed change from current law.........................	-2	-20	-61	-41	-37	-161	-322

Administration Proposal and Impact

The 2009 Budget proposes to amend the Federal Land Transaction Facilitation Act (FLTFA) by expanding the set of lands that the Department of the Interior (DOI) would be authorized to sell under the Act. It would also authorize additional uses of the funds generated from FLTFA land sales. Under the proposal, DOI would be able to retain 30 percent (plus administrative costs) of the proceeds from the sale of Bureau of Land Management (BLM) lands that have been identified for disposal in all BLM land use plans. The agency would be able to use a portion of the proceeds for restoration projects on BLM lands (in addition to the traditional use for land acquisition).

The proposal would return the remaining 70 percent of net proceeds to the Treasury, exclusive of BLM's administrative costs. In addition, DOI receipt retention would be capped at $60 million per year; all revenues in excess of this cap would be returned to the Treasury. This proposal will allow BLM more flexibility over which lands it sells, minimize the amount of Federal spending not subject to regular oversight through the appropriations process, and ensure that taxpayers benefit directly from these land sales.

Background

FLTFA was enacted by the Congress in 2000 to better rationalize BLM land ownership patterns and encourage the sale of lands that do little to contribute to the agency's mission. The Act authorizes the sale of BLM lands that have been classified as suitable for disposal under resource management plans in place at the time the Act was passed. Further, it allows the Department of the Interior to retain the proceeds from these sales to cover BLM's administrative costs for conducting the sales and to acquire other high-value non-Federal parcels within specially-designated areas such as national parks, refuges, and monuments.

FLTFA is set to expire in 2010. Reauthorization of an amended FLTFA authority in 2009 will facilitate continuity in BLM planning of future land sales and the allocation of the DOI share of proceeds from those sales to new land purchases or other conservation projects.

This policy proposal reflects the Administration's objections to Federal land sale bills that seek to retain the proceeds for State and local government use. The Administration believes that all taxpayers should benefit from the sale of Federal lands.

Department of the Interior: Mandatory Proposal
Eliminate Bureau of Land Management Range Improvement Fund

Funding Summary
(In millions of dollars)

	2009	2010	2011	2012	2013	2009-13	2009-18
Baseline outlays..................	--	--	--	--	--	--	--
Proposed change from current law.........................	-6	-9	-10	-10	-10	-45	-95

Administration Proposal and Impact

The 2009 Budget proposes to eliminate the Bureau of Land Management's (BLM's) range improvement fund, a mandatory fund derived primarily from the Federal share of receipts from fees charged for grazing on BLM public lands. Receipts would be redirected to the General Fund of the Treasury. The mandatory nature of the range improvement funding does not allow program managers to consider an array of spending options and shift funding toward higher priorities.

Under the Administration's proposal, BLM would retain the ability to fund range improvements to benefit wildlife within its appropriated budget. Also, private users who directly benefit from range improvements may be willing to share in these costs. Additional private investment could decrease the need for the Federal Government to fund these projects.

Background

BLM's Range Improvement program is funded from a combination of money from both appropriations and grazing fees received for allowing ranchers to graze livestock on public lands. These grazing fees compensate the public for the use of Federal lands for this purpose. Range improvements include vegetation projects, fencing, and livestock watering troughs.

Department of the Interior: Mandatory Proposal
Recover Pick-Sloan Project Cost

Funding Summary
(In millions of dollars)

	2009	2010	2011	2012	2013	2009-13	2009-18
Baseline outlays..................	-144	-145	-144	-144	-144	-721	-1,441
Proposed change from current law.........................	-23	-23	-23	-23	-23	-115	-230

Administration Proposal and Impact

The Budget proposes to re-allocate repayment of capital costs of the Pick-Sloan Missouri Basin Program. Power customers will be responsible for repayment of all construction from which they benefit, whereas to date they have only been responsible for a portion of it. This proposal will not impact services, and will ensure taxpayer investments are being repaid as intended, through a modest increase in power rates to the program's beneficiaries. This increase would be phased out when costs are repaid.

Background

This multipurpose, multi-agency (Reclamation, Corps of Engineers, and Western Area Power Administration) irrigation, flood control, and power generation program serves parts of ten States in the Midwest. Power customers have repaid the construction costs of most of the project, and annually reimburse Reclamation for its operating and maintenance (O&M) expenses on that portion of the project. However, several hundred million dollars of the program's hydropower and water storage capital costs were allocated to irrigators. Because the irrigation was never developed, the capital and O&M costs on this portion of the project are not being repaid to the Federal Government. Meanwhile, power customers have been using, but not paying for, the dams and reservoirs originally allocated to irrigation, and the price of the power has, therefore, been subsidized.

The Government successfully took similar cost re-allocation action for part of this project in the mid-1980s, with minimal impacts to power rates. Both the Government Accountability Office and the Department of the Interior's Office of the Inspector General have raised concerns that these costs are not being paid, and suggested that costs be re-allocated to power customers.

Department of Labor: Mandatory Proposal
Pension Benefit Guaranty Corporation

Funding Summary
(In millions of dollars)

	2009	2010	2011	2012	2013	2009-13	2009-18
Baseline outlays...................	-202	698	328	505	659	1,988	6,869
Proposed change from current law.........................	-380	-2,217	-2,093	-2,127	-2,056	-8,873	-18,514

Administration Proposal and Impact

The 2009 Budget proposes to restore the solvency of the Pension Benefit Guaranty Corporation (PBGC) by increasing the insurance premiums paid by underfunded pension plans. While the Pension Protection Act made significant structural changes to the retirement system, PBGC is still not solvent on a long-term basis. Further reforms are needed to address the $14 billion gap between PBGC's liabilities and its assets. If there is not enough money in the system to cover worker benefits, taxpayers are at risk for having to cover the shortfall.

The Budget proposes to give PBGC's Board the authority to raise premiums to produce the revenue necessary to meet expected future claims and retire PBGC's deficit over ten years. Proposed premium reforms will generate $18.5 billion over ten years, improving PBGC's financial condition and safeguarding the future retirement benefits of American workers.

Background

PBGC is a Federal Government corporation that insures the retirement incomes of the more than 44 million Americans in defined benefit pension plans. Under current law, the gap between PBGC's assets and liabilities—now $14 billion—is expected to grow over the next ten years. Large pension plan defaults over the past few years have considerably worsened the position of the PBGC and added a large number of beneficiaries to PBGC's rolls. PBGC is now responsible for paying the benefits of 1.2 million workers and retirees. PBGC premiums are currently far lower than what a private financial institution would charge for insuring the same risk. While the agency's deficit at 2007 year-end is a $5 billion improvement from 2006, its financial sustainability is threatened by its long-term exposure to loss and a flawed funding system. In addition, the Administration believes that the airline relief provisions in the Pension Protection Act of 2006, which forestalled the termination of airline plans in bankruptcy, simply postponed rather than eliminated losses, as it is likely that the airlines will eventually relapse and present a claim to the PBGC.

Department of Labor: Mandatory Proposal
Unemployment Insurance

Funding Summary
(In millions of dollars)

	2009	2010	2011	2012	2013	2009-13	2009-18
Baseline outlays..................	37,352	38,756	40,671	42,347	44,157	203,283	456,002
Proposed change from current law........................	---	-470	-504	-356	-362	-1,692	-3,632

Administration Proposal and Impact

The 2009 Budget proposes legislation to strengthen the financial integrity of the Unemployment Insurance (UI) system by reducing improper benefit payments and tax avoidance. The reforms will generate direct savings of $3.6 billion over 10 years and allow States to reduce their UI taxes by $2.1 billion. The Administration's proposal will boost States' ability to recover UI overpayments and deter tax evasion schemes by permitting them to use a portion of recovered funds to expand enforcement efforts in these areas and pay for private collection agencies. It will permit collection of delinquent UI overpayments and employer taxes through garnishment of Federal tax refunds. The proposal will also improve the accuracy of hiring data in the National Directory of New Hires, which would reduce overpayments.

These efforts to strengthen the financial integrity of the UI system will keep State UI taxes down and improve the solvency of the States' unemployment trust funds.

Background

The UI program was created in 1935 to provide temporary income support to workers who have lost their jobs through no fault of their own. The program is a Federal-State partnership. The States determine an unemployed worker's eligibility for UI benefits and pay the benefits with State-levied taxes on employers. The Federal Government provides grants to States for the program's administrative expenses, helps pay for extended unemployment benefits during recessions, and provides interest-bearing loans to States that run short of funds to pay UI benefits.

Improper benefit payments and tax avoidance are top management challenges for the UI program and serve to undermine the integrity of the program. Benefit overpayments were more than $3 billion in 2007. The Administration and the Congress have worked together to give the States new tools to reduce overpayments and decrease employer tax evasion. For example, the State Unemployment Tax Act (SUTA) Dumping Prevention Act of 2004 addressed the practice by unscrupulous employers of manipulating their UI tax rates, thereby shifting costs to other employers. That Act also gave State unemployment agencies access to the National Directory of New Hires so that they have more timely information to prevent UI claimants who have gone back to work from continuing to collect weekly benefits. The Budget's proposed reforms would supplement these reforms, giving States and the Federal Government more tools to reduce improper payments.

Department of Labor: Mandatory Proposal
Federal Employees' Compensation Program Act

Funding Summary
(In millions of dollars)

	2009	2010	2011	2012	2013	2009-13	2009-18
Baseline outlays....................	160	165	170	175	180	850	1,958
Proposed change from current law.........................	-10	-14	-21	-15	-12	-72	-288

Administration Proposal and Impact

The 2009 Budget reproposes legislation to update the Federal Employees' Compensation Act (FECA) program's benefit structure, adopt best practices of State workers' compensation systems, and strengthen return-to-work incentives. The proposed legislation would amend FECA to convert prospectively retirement-age beneficiaries to a retirement annuity-level benefit, impose an up-front waiting period for benefits (as is done in every State workers' compensation system), streamline claims processing, permit the Department of Labor (DOL) to recapture compensation costs from responsible third parties, authorize DOL to cross-match FECA records with Social Security records to reduce improper payments, and make other changes to improve and update FECA. The program has not been substantially updated since 1974.

The table above reflects net savings to the FECA account and does not include projected reductions in Federal agencies' payments for FECA benefits paid to their employees. On a government-wide basis, these reforms are expected to produce 10-year savings of more than $377 million.

Background

Administered by DOL, FECA covers nearly three million Federal employees, providing wage-replacement and medical benefits to those workers who suffer occupational injury or disease. FECA benefits are paid by DOL, which is then reimbursed by Federal agencies for benefits paid to their employees. FECA pays up to 75 percent of the individual's basic pay, adjusted annually based on the Consumer Price Index. Under current law, individuals can receive FECA benefits indefinitely, as long as their injury or illness diminishes their wage-earning capacity. FECA benefits typically exceed Federal retirement benefits, a fact that entices individuals to remain on FECA beyond the point when they otherwise would have retired.

Department of the Treasury: Mandatory Proposal
Payment Transaction Integrity

Funding Summary
(In millions of dollars)

	2009	2010	2011	2012	2013	2009-13	2009-18
Baseline outlays..................	---	---	---	---	---	---	---
Proposed change from current law........................	-53	-56	-60	-64	-68	-301	-717

Administration Proposal and Impact

The Budget proposes to allow the Federal Government to trace and recover Federal payments sent electronically to the wrong account. The proposal would revise an existing exception to the Right to Financial Privacy Act of 1978 so that improper electronic payments and improperly directed Treasury checks can be traced and recovered. As examples, this proposal would allow for the disclosure of financial information so that misdirected and/or improper electronic tax refunds, Thrift Savings Plan withdrawals, and Office of Personnel Management annuity payments could be traced and recovered, saving taxpayers from the cost of making payments to those not entitled to receive them. This proposal would also require Treasury to take the responsible step of verifying the ownership of a bank account before electronically debiting the account to collect funds owed to the Government. This proposal is part of the Administration's Eliminating Improper Payments Initiative that thus far has reduced the Government-wide error rate for the 30 programs that first reported in 2004 from 4.25 percent to 3.07 percent.

Background

The Right to Financial Privacy Act of 1978 (the Act) generally prohibits financial institutions from disclosing financial records to Federal agencies unless subpoenaed. While the Act contains various exceptions to the prohibition (e.g., disclosure of financial records is permitted to the Social Security Administration and the Railroad Retirement Board for the proper administration of these programs), there is no exception that permits disclosure of records to the Federal Government for purposes of tracing or recovering improper payments and collections. For example, if a Federal payment has been issued to the account of an ineligible recipient, the financial institution to which the payment was issued is generally barred from disclosing the necessary information to recover the payment.

Department of the Treasury: Mandatory Proposal
Modernize Cash Investment Practices

Funding Summary
(In millions of dollars)

	2009	2010	2011	2012	2013	2009-13	2009-18
Baseline outlays	---	---	---	---	---	---	---
Proposed change from current law	-10	-10	-10	-10	-10	-50	-100

Administration Proposal and Impact

The 2009 Budget proposes to give the Secretary of the Treasury the ability to manage the Government's excess operating cash more efficiently. This initiative would enable the Secretary of the Treasury to employ more effective techniques for investing the excess cash balances, when needed and in the Government's best interests, allowing Treasury to increase investment capacity, reduce risk, and improve earnings on investments. Once fully implemented, this initiative is expected to increase, by approximately $10 million annually, the interest earnings on the Treasury's investment of excess cash. Such earnings would be deposited in the general fund of the Treasury.

Background

Currently, the Treasury Tax and Loan (TT&L) statute (31 U.S.C. 323) is the authority under which the Department of the Treasury may invest excess operating cash. Under the current TT&L program, the Department of the Treasury allows certain depositary institutions, principally banks, savings and loan associations, and credit unions, to hold Treasury funds for a period of time in return for interest earnings at a rate prescribed by the Secretary.

While the TT&L system has been, and continues to be, a useful investment tool, this proposal recognizes that the market has changed since the TT&L program was instituted in 1977, and that the repurchase market is a safe and appropriate investment option for Treasury's operating cash. It provides an opportunity for the Department of the Treasury to engage in repurchase transactions with acceptable parties, which will provide a better rate of return than the Department of the Treasury currently receives under the TT&L program.

Department of the Treasury: Mandatory Proposal
Debt Collection Initiative - Eliminate the 10-year Statute-of-Limitations on the Collection of Non-Tax Debt Owed to Federal Agencies

Funding Summary
(In millions of dollars)

	2009	2010	2011	2012	2013	2009-13	2009-18
Baseline outlays...................	---	---	---	---	---	---	---
Proposed change from current law........................	-15	-8	-8	-8	-8	-47	-87

Administration Proposal and Impact

This proposal would eliminate the 10-year statute of limitations period applicable to the offset of Federal non-tax payments. These Federal payments are offset in order to collect debts such as delinquent loan payments due to the Small Business Administration, unpaid fines and penalties due to the Occupational Health and Safety Administration, or other debts owed to Federal agencies. Under current law, Federal payments made to payees (e.g., vendors, beneficiaries) who are delinquent on their debt to the Federal Government cannot be offset if the debt has been outstanding for more than 10 years (student loan debts are an exception since they can be collected without regard to time limitations). The proposal would ensure that all delinquent obligations to the Federal Government can be collected by offset without regard to any Federal or State statutory, regulatory, or administrative limitation on the period within which debts may be collected. The ability to pursue collection indefinitely would be tempered by Government-wide regulations that set forth standards for when it is and is not appropriate to continue collection. Such standards are intended to ensure that the Federal Government's debt collection efforts are directed toward those with the ability to pay.

The proposal includes language clarifying that this change applies to current debts that are or become ten years delinquent and not just to debts that may still be delinquent 10 years from the time this proposal is enacted.

Background

The Financial Management Service debt collection offset process collects delinquent non-tax debts owed to Federal agencies by private entities by reducing tax refunds and other Federal payments (e.g., benefits payments, vendor payments, and Federal wages through garnishment) made to those entities. In 2007, the debt collection program collected a record $3.76 billion in delinquent debt. In 2003, the Debt Collection program received an Effective rating on an evaluation using OMB's Program Assessment Rating Tool (PART). As a result of the PART analysis, the 2005 Budget proposed initiatives to increase opportunities to collect delinquent debt owed to Federal agencies. Several of the proposals have since been enacted into law.

Department of Veterans Affairs: Mandatory Proposal
Medical Care

Funding Summary
(In millions of dollars)

	2009	2010	2011	2012	2013	2009-13	2009-18
Baseline outlays..	---	---	---	---	---	---	---
Proposed change from current law:							
Adopt Third-Party Insurance Co-Payment Offset..............	-44	-44	-44	-43	-43	-218	-420
Charge Medical Care Enrollment Fees for Non-Disabled							
Higher-Income Veterans and Increase Pharmacy							
Co-Payments to Align with Other Health Care Plans....	-335	-421	-414	-464	-483	-2,117	-4,796
Total..	-379	-465	-458	-507	-526	-2,335	-5,216

Administration Proposal and Impact

The 2009 Budget proposes new or higher fees for non-disabled higher-income (PL 7/8) veterans. The new user fees refocus the Department of Veterans Affairs' (VA) resources on its core medical care mission of serving veterans returning from combat, those with military disabilities, lower incomes, and special needs. (Existing medical care collections offset discretionary spending, while the proposed fees are mandatory and will not reduce the medical care appropriation request which has been made in full.)

The three user fee proposals (which are the same as in the 2008 Budget) are:

- Pharmacy Co-Payment: Co-payments would increase from $8 to $15 for all PL 7/8 veterans, more closely aligning VA with other private and public health care plans.

- Income-based Enrollment Fee: PL 7/8 veterans would pay an annual enrollment fee of $250 with households incomes from $50,000 to $74,999, $500 with incomes from $75,000 to $99,999, and $750 with incomes equal to or greater than $100,000.

- Insurance Co-Payment: Technical correction legislative language will ensure that current co-pays are charged to all eligible veterans equally and not reduced if a veteran has health insurance. (Note: no fees are ever charged for treating service-related disabilities).

Background

The VA medical care program will provide care to nearly 6 million veterans, over 333,000 of which will be returning from combat in Operation Enduring Freedom and Operation Iraqi Freedom.

Commodity Futures Trading Commission: Mandatory Proposal Futures and Options Transaction Fee

Funding Summary
(In millions of dollars)

	2009	2010	2011	2012	2013	2009-13	2009-18
Proposed change from current law................................	-96	-100	-103	-107	-111	-517	-1,130

Administration Proposal and Impact

The 2009 Budget proposes to collect a fee on the settlement of contracts on commodity futures, options on futures, and other transactions cleared by derivatives clearing organizations. The Commodity Futures Trading Commission (CFTC) is the only Federal financial regulator that does not derive its funding from the specialized entities it regulates. Since the CFTC's efforts to ensure the transparency and resiliency of futures and options exchanges provide clear benefits to market participants, it is appropriate for those participants to at least partially offset or contribute toward the cost of providing those programs. The fees would be set at a level to equal the costs to the taxpayer of funding CFTC's Market Oversight and Clearing & Intermediary Oversight functions, about $96 million during 2009. Such fees are already imposed on futures exchanges to fund the programs of the futures industry's self-regulatory organization. The proceeds from the fees would be returned to the general fund of the Treasury and would offset the deficit impact of continuing to fund the CFTC's operations through direct appropriations.

Background

The CFTC ensures the integrity and effectiveness of the U.S. futures and options markets through administration of the Commodity Exchange Act of 1936, as amended. Fees would facilitate increases in CFTC's proposed oversight activities, which have been held generally constant by annual appropriations limitations while trading volume has increased six-fold over the last decade. The notional value of contracts under the regulatory oversight of the CFTC is greater than $4 trillion per day.

Environmental Protection Agency: Mandatory Proposal
Pesticide User Fees

Funding Summary
(In millions of dollars)

	2009	2010	2011	2012	2013	2009-13	2009-18
Proposed change from current law................................	-48	-48	-47	-47	-37	-227	-426

Administration Proposal and Impact

The 2009 Budget proposes to collect an additional $48 million in pesticide user fees, which would cover approximately 34 percent of the costs of pesticide activities in the Environmental Protection Agency (EPA) in 2009. Under current law, less than 13 percent of the costs will be covered by fees. The 2009 Budget proposes to:

- Increase collections of currently authorized pesticide user fees;
- Eliminate the Pesticide Registration Improvement Renewal Act (PRIRA) prohibition on a tolerance fee and collect it in 2009;
- Eliminate the budget floor in PRIRA.

The total cost of the EPA's pesticides programs in 2009 is estimated to be $221 million. Of the total, $63 million (28 percent) will come from two fees currently charged to pesticide registrants for registration and reregistration activities. The Administration has long maintained that the bulk of the costs associated with EPA's pesticide activities should be covered by fees because pesticide registrants receive direct benefits from EPA's services, similar to the policy used at FDA, which charges fees to cover the cost of approving new drugs.

Background

EPA's pesticides activities include the registration and reregistration of pesticides, the establishment and reassessment of pesticide tolerances, and various field activities that support the implementation of registered pesticides requirements. Registration, reregistration, and tolerance work are complex, technically intense activities that involve scientific risk assessments and evaluation of human health and environmental impacts. EPA currently collects fees from entities seeking to register their pesticides and from entities with existing pesticides registered for use in the United States, as authorized by the Pesticide Registration Improvement Renewal Act of 2007. However PRIRA also prohibits EPA from collecting other statutorily required fees such as those for setting tolerances.

Environmental Protection Agency: Mandatory Proposal
Pre-Manufacture Notification (PMN) Fee

Funding Summary
(In millions of dollars)

	2009	2010	2011	2012	2013	2009-13	2009-18
Proposed change from current law..................................	-4	-8	-8	-8	-8	-36	-76

Administration Proposal and Impact

The 2009 Budget proposes to eliminate the $2,500 cap on the Pre-Manufacture Notification (PMN) fee to allow the Environmental Protection Agency (EPA) to recover a greater portion of the cost of the program. This proposal is consistent with government-wide efforts to appropriately align program costs to those who benefit directly from such services.

Background

EPA reviews new chemicals and their intended uses to ensure that they are not harmful to human health and the environment. Manufacturers must submit a pre-manufacture notice to EPA for these chemicals. Since 1999, EPA has collected limited fees to defray part of the cost of reviewing and processing these notices. Currently, the fees collected cover approximately one-quarter of the program costs. TSCA currently limits the fee amount that can be charged to manufacturers at a level which does not adequately cover the cost of the PMN program.

Federal Communications Commission: Mandatory Proposal Spectrum License Fee Authority

Funding Summary
(In millions of dollars)

	2009	2010	2011	2012	2013	2009-13	2009-18
Proposed change from current law...........................	-150	-300	-300	-400	-450	-1,600	-4,081

Administration Proposal and Impact

To continue to promote efficient spectrum use, the 2009 Budget proposes to provide the Federal Communications Commission (FCC) with new authority to use other economic mechanisms, such as fees, as a spectrum management tool. The Commission would be authorized to set user fees on previously un-auctioned spectrum licenses based on public-interest and spectrum-management principles. Fees would be phased in over time as part of an ongoing rulemaking process to determine the appropriate application and level for fees.

Background

The FCC began auctioning communications spectrum licenses in 1994. While most commercial spectrum licenses are assigned using auctions, fee authority would enable the FCC to ensure that the economic value of spectrum is reflected in the limited category of commercial licenses that are given away non-competitively. This additional economic tool would help to reduce market distortions by bringing greater parity to spectrum license acquisition costs, thus promoting greater efficiency in the use of spectrum resources. In addition, since the FCC's licensing activities benefit a specific identifiable group of commercial firms, it is appropriate that these firms be charged for the rights to use spectrum resources.

Federal Communications Commission: Mandatory Proposal
Ancillary Terrestrial Component License Fee

Funding Summary
(In millions of dollars)

	2009	2010	2011	2012	2013	2009-13	2009-18
Proposed change from current law.................................	-60	-100	-125	-125	-125	-535	-1,160

Administration Proposal and Impact

The 2009 Budget proposes to enable fees to be used to manage the land-based component of hybrid terrestrial-satellite communications networks, such as the Ancillary Terrestrial Component to Mobile Satellite Services. Currently, the authority to use the land-based component of these hybrid networks is given away to companies that have received licenses for the satellite component. The use of fees on the Ancillary Terrestrial Component of these hybrid networks will help to ensure that the radio spectrum is assigned efficiently and effectively, prevent windfalls at taxpayer expense, and promote fair competition in wireless services.

Background

The Federal Communications Commission (FCC) uses auctions to assign most new commercial licenses for use of the radio spectrum. These spectrum license auctions have helped to promote new wireless services, as well as competition and economic growth in the telecommunications industry. However, auctions are prohibited as an assignment mechanism for certain services, including international satellite communications services such as Mobile Satellite Services (MSS), due to the multilateral coordination needed to secure consistent orbital locations and spectrum across national boundaries.

The growing convergence of satellite and terrestrial communications gives rise to the need to ensure spectrum management frameworks are updated. For example, in 2003, the FCC decided to permit MSS providers to apply for terrestrial authorization (i.e., service relying on traditional cell towers) on the spectrum used for satellite services, which is called an Ancillary Terrestrial Component (ATC). Under current policy, this ATC authority is given away free of charge, though it allows providers to compete with terrestrial wireless service providers that have purchased their licenses at auction.

This proposal would help to ensure that these hybrid land-satellite communications networks are managed in an efficient and effective manner.

Federal Communications Commission: Mandatory Proposal
Extend Spectrum Auction Authority

Funding Summary
(In millions of dollars)

	2009	2010	2011	2012	2013	2009-13	2009-18
Proposed change from current law..................................	---	---	---	-200	-200	-400	-1,400

Administration Proposal and Impact

The 2009 Budget proposes to extend the Federal Communications Commission's (FCC's) auction authority indefinitely. Auction of spectrum licenses has proved to be an efficient, fair, and transparent approach to allocating this resource and has helped ensure that taxpayers receive fair market value. Collections are estimated to be $200 million per year beginning in 2012.

Background

FCC began auctioning communications spectrum licenses in 1994. These auctions have been widely recognized as an effective and successful approach to allocating licenses. The Deficit Reduction Act of 2005 extended FCC's authority to auction spectrum licenses through fiscal year 2011.

Federal Communications Commission: Mandatory Proposal
Domestic Satellite Spectrum License Auctions

Funding Summary
(In millions of dollars)

	2009	2010	2011	2012	2013	2009-13	2009-18
Proposed change from current law.................................	-100	-100	-75	-20	-15	-310	-343

Administration Proposal and Impact

The 2009 Budget proposes to ensure that spectrum licenses for predominantly domestic satellite services are assigned efficiently and effectively through competitive bidding at auctions. Services such as Direct Broadcast Satellite (satellite TV) and Satellite Digital Audio Radio Services (satellite radio) were assigned by auction prior to a 2005 court decision that questioned this practice on technical grounds. By clarifying through legislation that auctions of licenses for these domestic satellite services are authorized, prior policy of the Federal Communications Commission (FCC) will be restored, and taxpayers will avoid the giveaway of valuable spectrum assets.

Background

The FCC uses auctions to assign most new commercial licenses for the use of the radio spectrum. These spectrum license auctions have helped to promote new wireless services, as well as competition and economic growth. However, the FCC's authority to auction spectrum for Direct Broadcast Services was recently limited by a U.S. Court of Appeals decision. If the FCC's authority to auction such licenses is not clarified legislatively, the agency will be unable to utilize this efficient market-based assignment mechanism, and will instead be required to give away spectrum through a regulatory assignment process.

Federal Communications Commission: Mandatory Proposal
Telecommunications Development Fund Termination

Funding Summary
(In millions of dollars)

	2009	2010	2011	2012	2013	2009-13	2009-18
Baseline outlays..................	6	7	7	7	7	34	69
Proposed change from current law.........................	-6	-7	-7	-7	-7	-34	-69

Administration Proposal and Impact

The 2009 Budget proposes to terminate the Telecommunications Development Fund (TDF). The fund has had no demonstrated effect in meeting its statutory goals, and eliminating the fund would have no significant impact on the telecommunications sector.

Background

The Telecommunications Fund was created by the Congress in 1996 with the mandate to finance small businesses in the telecommunications sector, help develop new technologies, and promote universal telecommunications service. It started operations in 1998 as an equity investment venture capital fund focusing on early-stage companies. Over the years, the fund has been solely capitalized by the Federal Government by retaining the interest earned on deposits made by bidders in FCC spectrum auctions. Between 1998 and 2009, TDF will have received approximately $110 million in interest on these deposits.

The savings shown above represent the Fund's administrative costs. The Fund's investment track record has been mixed, and the Administration believes that TDF is unnecessary in light of the large sums of investment capital available through the private sector.

Office of Personnel Management: Mandatory Proposal
Federal Employees Health Benefits Program

Funding Summary
(In millions of dollars)

	2009	2010	2011	2012	2013	2009-13	2009-18
Baseline outlays..................	37,640	40,403	43,368	46,496	50,092	217,999	529,693
Proposed change from current law........................	-40	-147	-248	-327	-403	-1,165	-3,675

Administration Proposal and Impact

The 2009 Budget proposes reforms to the FEHBP with the goal of providing more choices, improving quality of care, increasing equity in benefits, and reducing costs for FEHBP enrollees as well as the Federal Government. This proposal would allow the Service Benefit Plan (Blue Cross/Blue Shield or BCBS) as well as the Indemnity Benefit Plan (IBP) to offer more than two levels of benefits to provide greater incentives to both FEHBP enrollees and health plans to reduce costs and improve quality. This proposal would yield savings from decreased Government contributions to health plans.

Background

Allowing the Service Benefit Plan (BCBS) as well as the IBP to offer more than two levels of benefits would provide more options to enrollees and advance the Administration's goal of promoting High Deductible Health Plans and Health Savings Accounts. At present, the Service Benefit Plan and the IBP Plan are limited by statute to just two levels of benefits. Last year, the Administration transmitted the amendment to allow BCBS to provide more than two levels of benefits; the Congress took no action. The proposal would permit not only BCBS but also the IBP to offer more than two levels of benefits. Although there is no IBP carrier available at present, OPM's proposal would provide a level playing field to the IBP when there is one.

www.ingramcontent.com/pod-product-compliance
Lightning Source LLC
Chambersburg PA
CBHW081824280526
45789CB00007B/2338